SO WHAT DO' YOU THINK?

KEITH DRURY

Copyright © 1998 by Wesleyan Publishing House
All Rights Reserved
Published by Wesleyan Publishing House
Indianapolis, Indiana 46250
Printed in the United States of America
ISBN 0-89827-190-8

TABLE OF CONTENTS

FOREWORD

This book is not a Bible study. It is a collection of essays designed to provoke the reader into thinking about important subjects facing the church today. It is easy to read, but not a "quick read." Why? Because the reader needs to think through the issues outlined in many of these essays. I have not so much told you what to think as to outline a position, then ask a half-dozen questions to help you hammer out your own position on these subjects.

You may agree or disagree with my essays, but that is not what is so important. Rather, my hope is that you will use each essay as a diving board to get into the pool of deeper thinking on the subject. Wherever you wind up on these issues, I will have succeeded if this book gets you thinking.

One more thing. I have carefully planted questions at the end of most chapters to prod you toward the Scriptures. It is not my intent to dig out the Bible's answers to current issues for you, but rather to steer you to the Bible where you can find your own answers. This book may ask the questions, but the Bible has the answers. If you use this book in a group discussion, make sure you have more than a gabfest in which everybody shares personal opinions and displays ignorance. Somebody needs to lead the group, directing it to the Word of God — which is the primary tiebreaker among the various opinions in the church.

From worship styles, homosexuality, and tongues to eternal security and dealing with multilevel salesmen in the church, this book deals with some pretty controversial issues. But isn't that where we need the most thinking? Many of the essays published here first appeared as a weekly Internet column on religious matters. Several ignited hundreds of responses by e-mail. Thank you to those loyal weekly readers whose responses have helped me revise and even improve my original material.

And thanks most to you. A writer is no writer without readers. I hope you'll have an exciting read. Take your time and be sure to think for yourself about many of these issues. God is not afraid for you to use your mind to think more about His church and His work. This is in fact how we get the mind of God on things.

Keith Drury
Marion, Indiana
1998

TOTAL ABSTINENCE . . . I'LL DRINK TO THAT!

I don't drink alcohol, not even socially. To some that makes me a legalist. To many of my "Boomer" peers, who think it is totally uncool to be a teetotaler, that makes me a conservative. In the interest of being more popular with my liberated Boomer peers and accepted as cool by the Generation X crowd, should I reconsider my hard-line position on alcohol? Maybe I should loosen up a bit and chug-a-lug along with the rest of 'em so that "I might by all means save some"(1 Cor. 9:22 KJV).

After considerable (sober) thought on the matter I've decided that I am *not* going to start drinking . . . I'll stick with "total abstinence." I know many of you will be disappointed that I'm still up here on the wagon, but I remain unconvinced of alcohol's usefulness. I'm sure you wonder why and are breathlessly waiting for my rationale. I hear that many nowadays are seeking a good rationale for total abstinence (not really). But just in case any of you hunger for sound argument, here are my own reasons for sticking with Diet Coke® (except for an occasional shot of that nite-time-sneezy-stuffy-nose-cold-so-you-can-rest-medicine). Here's why I don't drink:

1. I Don't Need It.

I realize that alcohol is the social lubricant of the American business culture. And I know that when Evangelicals' clientele came from skid row this was a clear-cut issue — reformed drunks know exactly where to draw the line. But we've moved uptown now. Or rather to the edge of town. Evangelicals don't run many missions anymore — we let Roman Catholics and the mainline churches do that. Instead, we cater to the dire needs of suburbia and have been populating our churches with social climbers and "quality people." These folk use alcohol like their DayTimers™ — as a social and political tool to grease their career tracks. So of course, following our newfound market share, most Evangelicals will eventually come to approve the drinking habits of our wealthy patrons. The customer is often right.

In fact, my own denomination will probably "open up" and "abandon legalism" sooner or later, adopting a more contemporary and pragmatic approach to alcohol. Not right away, but eventually I suspect. After all, "some of our best people drink." They also tithe. But even if my church legalizes drinking, I still won't drink. I just don't need it. It would take more than alcohol to grease my career track.

2. Social Protest.

This is really the major reason I don't drink. To me, the alcohol industry is merely a group of drug pushers dressed up in suits. I think they are pushers running their dirty little industry at the expense of other people's pain. So I boycott them. Sure, I know it won't break 'em. I don't do it to run them out of business. I do it to keep from supporting them. I do it for me, not against them. Yeah, I know, their Super Bowl frogs were cute several years ago, and their "I love you maaaaan" commercials were delightful. But when you strip away all the ad-man cleverness, they are simply liquid drug traffickers and I won't support them. It doesn't matter to me that their customers want the drug, or even that it is legal. I just boycott them. Not far from where I live and write in Indianapolis, there is a huge chain of liquor stores which purposely preys on poor people. I don't care if the owner of this chain dresses in classy $500 suits and attends a respectable church. He's no better in my mind than a street corner drug pusher. I'm an old hippie who went without California lettuce for several years to support the migrant workers. That boycott was about fair wages. This is about destroyed families, ruined livers and perpetuating poverty. I know my abstinence won't change things, but I do it anyway. This is one industry that introduces plenty of hell on earth. So, I just boycott them.

3. Abstinence Is a Clear Line.

OK, OK, I know the Bible doesn't forbid alcohol. It condemns drunkenness. But drunkenness is a foggy thing. When does a social drinker get drunk? After one drink? Three? Six? A dozen? See? I can't say for sure. Most Bible students agree that drunkenness is sin, but when does the drinker get drunk? In college I wondered what it would be like to get drunk. So I hustled a jug of wine out of a Jewish friend's party, pulled off the road in Allentown, Pennsylvania and chugged down the entire jug. Discarding the empty jug in a nearby trash can, I then drove 40 miles home. Was I drunk? Who knows? I didn't know. That's my point. Since then, I haven't touched it at all. Total abstinence is an easier line for me to enforce on myself. If drunkenness is sin, and therefore I shouldn't get drunk, how am I going to know when I've crossed the line? Carry my own breathilizer?

4. My Denomination.

I am a member of a denomination that "requires" teetotaling (as much as any denomination can "require" anything anymore). Indeed, many (American) Evangelicals have a similar heritage. For 150 years, four generations of folk in my denomination have pretty well agreed that total abstinence is the way to go. Hey, I don't want to toss that overboard without a bit more thought. I like my denomination on most days, so even if I wanted to drink, if abstinence has been important to the people in this church for 150 years, I can think about it a little while longer.

5. Church History.

Not that I am locked into the past, I recognize that the church has not always been against alcohol. In fact, given 2000 years of history, abstinence (for the masses) is a rather recent notion. But then again, so is opposition to slavery and the notion of ordaining women. So while I respect Christian tradition, I am not locked into it — especially if the thing in question being eliminated from society would benefit all of us. That was true of slavery. Is there anyone who would argue it could not also be true of alcohol?

6. For the Kids.

I can't imagine drinking — even in moderation — then being hypocritical enough to tell kids to abstain. "Hey, kids, do what I say, not what I do." Suuuuuuure! I don't want kids to drink — my kids or yours — so I don't drink. It's that simple.

Now I suspect some of you fine readers will want to broaden my thinking and help me understand how a good stiff drink each day will delay my heart attack by three months and 13 days. Thank you very much for your concern. But, I'll give up eggs instead.

Will most evangelical churches loosen up their tradition of total abstinence in the coming twenty years? Should they?

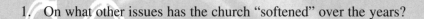

1. On what other issues has the church "softened" over the years?

2. Do you think this common rule of alcohol abstention will also be dropped in the future? Should it? Why or why not?

3. What reasons for teetotaling that the writer missed would you add?

4. What arguments might be given for softening up the church's stance on alcohol?

5. Where would you go in the Bible to support your position either way?

6 So, what is your own personal position on this matter?

WHO IS YOUR GOD #2?

In the spring of each year the church — especially men of the church — commemorate one of the great high celebrations of the year. It offers all the great themes of human emotion: agony, commitment, love, suffering, sacrifice and victory.

I'm writing about the Final Four NCAA Division I playoffs, not Easter. A while back the playoffs actually coincided with Easter weekend, making it difficult for many men to focus on the resurrection of Christ. Though there is never a game on Easter Sunday itself, if it *were* held Sunday morning at 11:00 a.m., many men would have to choose on that day which god they would serve. You and I both know which god would come in second for many men — and a few women, too.

Why is it that most of us Evangelicals are so silent about the powerful grip the god of sports has on American men? We attempt to help men break their habits of drinking and smoking. Some denominations even try to persuade their men to quit the Masons because of the pseudo-religious nature of secret societies. But we say little about the most powerful competitive god of all — American Sports.

Sociologist-turned-General-Superintendent John Williams (Ohio Yearly Meeting of Friends) warned us 25 years ago in *Eternity* magazine. He argued that sports would eventually edge out Christian commitment for evangelical men. He predicted the future for many men. Sports is a great religion! It has all of the characteristics of a good competitor for Christianity. It gradually captures a man's mind, heart and soul until he gives himself over to it with total commitment and fidelity. Left to its own, the god of Sports will fully possess a man and force the true God into second place. God doesn't like to have other gods before Him.

But it's no wonder this god has made such headway in our culture. It offers so much that is similar to the real thing. We have our holy seasons of Christmas, Easter and Pentecost, but the god of Sports offers the World Series, the Super Bowl and the Final Four. Few men think, talk and meditate on Pentecost as much as they do the Super Bowl. A ticket to these high holy day events is harder to purchase than a medieval indulgence. If you aren't rich, you must gather before the Television, which is like the Cathedral's Leper's Peep of 500 years ago. The really dedicated adherents of the god of Sports memorize and recite the Mighty Acts of the saints, now canonized into their respective halls of fame. Some fans even take pilgrimages to these hallowed halls to admire the wax figures of the saints. Many fans collect trading cards like holy icons. Sports has its relics too — footballs, baseballs, bats, uniforms and basketballs displayed in glass cases in these hushed and holy halls. There are mysterious rituals like face-painting and end-zone dances. Hey, Sports has all the elements of a great religion! Sports offers high emotion, stories of grit and determination, pain and sacrifice, victory and defeat. And it all occurs in a gigantic structure in the center of town — reminiscent of medieval insistence that the local cathedral be the highest building in town — thus projecting its importance and might.

Some churches don't fight the competition from the Sports god. Some, like Solomon, even bring it into the church, fashioning a syncretistic amalgam. I admit that most church folk have never thought of Sports as a competing god. (Well, many women have.) We've heard so many speakers who worship at both shrines that we assume the two religions are compatible. And, perhaps to an extent, they are. Perhaps God doesn't mind us keeping a backup god hidden in our footlocker. But when the Sports god begins to take *first* place in the life of a man (or woman), it is time for ministers to honestly call a god a god.

1. Has the writer overblown the influence of sports on the American male?

2. What does it take to make a thing a "god" in one's life?

3. What are acceptable and sensible hobbies that fall short of being a "god" in one's life?

4. What other things are easily promoted into a "god" among today's church attendees?

5. What do you know about the competing "gods" in Bible times which relates to this issue?

6. What are some signs that sports — or anything else, for that matter — is competing with God in a person's life?

7. What practical hints would you give to "put sports in its place" in a person's life?

THE WORSHIP WARS

3

War and worship don't go together. At least they shouldn't. But in many churches today they do! Want to start a firestorm? Changing doctrine might not do it; changing worship styles will. But "worship wars" aren't new. After all, the first recorded murder was committed over worship styles.

In my life I've come through two worship wars . . . thus, I've experienced three worship styles. While this is just my own personal experience, I suspect it may reflect others too. And though there are some churches who, like the Amish, have "frozen in" one particular worship style and refuse all change, I suspect many churches have gone through the same two major revolutions I've experienced. The three worship styles in my life have been:

1. Holiness Campmeeting Worship (1945-1965)

This form of worship dominated the 1950s and early 1960s in my denomination. Services were upbeat, singing was robust (even boisterous at times), and gospel songs prevailed. Choruses were common — almost every church had yellow "Let's Sing" chorus brochures in every pew. (Millions were given away free by an alcohol-free insurance company.) The piano dominated the song service with a style called "evangelistic playing." The "song service" was led by a "song leader" who often sweated profusely as he whipped up the enthusiasm. Actually, he was half song leader half cheerleader. Sometimes people clapped as they sang, using their "instrument of ten strings." In this style of service the congregation was the choir, and the song leader called for them to "sing

it again" or even divided the group up into parts. If the song leader had a trombone he often grabbed it mid-song and blared along, revving up the congregation's fervor. It was an electric atmosphere and singing was loud and strong in our churches with flat ceilings.

But everything didn't happen on the "platform" in the campmeeting style of worship. The laity participated too. There was often a "testimony time" in which individuals gave personal reports on their spiritual progress or just gave praise to the Lord for something that had happened to them that week. There were often "prayer requests," with one layperson after another standing to explain a personal prayer need or to request prayer from someone else. When the entire group finally did go to prayer, many often knelt at the pews. Several people would often pray one after another in a "season of prayer." Sometimes they "lifted" in prayer — which produced a simultaneous chorus of prayer (which probably sounded like tongues-speaking to outsiders).

Sometimes there was a mass "moving" when people "shouted" or "ran the aisles" as they "got blessed." Sometimes this filled up the entire service so that "the preacher didn't get a chance to preach." (This was considered good.) The laymen were highly involved, often punctuating a sermon or song with a hardy "Amen!" or "Hallelujah!" to show their support.

The whole atmosphere would be considered quite "charismatic" today. It was exciting. Even outsiders came to church to watch. And sometimes they "got saved" at an "altar call" after being "under conviction." It worked. People liked it. As for worship, this generation had "got it right" — they knew how to "do" worship the way they liked it. Things, however, were about to change.

2. Respectable Half-Mainline Worship (1965-1980)

By the mid 1960s and early 1970s, an increasing number of people in my denomination either already were or had become middle-class professional types. In addition, the holiness movement reacted so strongly against the charismatic movement that we repressed anything "leaning charismatic," even if it was in our own past. The boisterous campmeeting style began to embarrass our "pastors" (who had been called "preachers" up to that time). A revolution was in the wind.

Gradually the noisy, uncontrolled, lay-driven, wildfire campmeeting style of worship was displaced by a more respectable style of worship. Organs were installed or made more dominant. Choirs were organized and robes were purchased. An "order of service" emerged — against much opposition ("you are putting constraints on the Spirit"). The "bulletin" emerged with a printed order of worship. The "pastoral prayer" gradually replaced the "season of prayer" and testimonies started to fade away.

Hymns became the general fodder for singing and the doxology showed up here and there. Sure, once in a while an old-timer would shout or wave a handkerchief, but gradually this too passed . . . when the old-timer passed away. The whole revolution created an atmosphere of professional respectability which no longer embarrassed us.

At my denomination's general conference a minister read a prepared prayer word-for-word. It was praised as "a beautiful prayer — the kind a general superintendent ought to pray." (He was indeed elected a general.)

By the end of the 1970s this revolution was over in most places. Worship styles had changed radically. The 1965-75 "worship wars" were over. Respectable worship had won. The change had been accomplished in spite of the strong resistance of the "traditionalists," who wanted to keep the campmeeting style (which they could sometimes still get a taste of once a year — at campmeeting, where else?).

As for worship, this now middle-aged generation figured they had finally "got it right." They knew how to "do" worship the way they liked it — "decently and in order." But this "new" worship style would not rule for long. Another revolution was in the wind.

3. "Contemporary" Worship (1980-1995[?])

No sooner had the "half-mainline worship" of their parents taken hold, than a whole crop of Baby Boomers came along with their own ideas of worship. We called it "contemporary" worship. (With typical conceit we assumed all other styles of worship were now out-of-date.) Out went hymnals and hymns. In came "praise choruses" — not on yellow "Let's Sing" sheets this time, but projected on a screen with an overhead or slide projector. The piano was replaced by a keyboard. If we could, we got together a "pit band" (or at least some pit band wannabees).

The song leader (who by now was far removed from the campmeeting cheerleader and was merely a number-caller) was replaced by a "praise team" of good-looking men and women to help us sing. The bulletin was still in service, but the real schedule was a minute-by-minute sheet used by the pastor, worship leader and sound man to manage "excellence in worship" — even right down to "planned spontaneity." Spotlights were fixed to metal bars running across the ceiling, and drama was introduced in place of some congregational singing.

The old "cantatas" were replaced by souped-up "Living Christmas Tree" programs which, in some cases, rivaled any live show in town. We borrowed "clapping-while-singing" from the charismatics (though we never can do it quite as well).

Then along came a young pastor from the Chicago suburbs with the "seeker service" idea — an adapted version of "contemporary worship" but designed for the unchurched. He was widely half-copied by many full-Boomers as we adapted our services more and more to a non-participatory event for watching.

By the early 1990s many pastors in their 30s and 40s had fully introduced this new style of worship. The war was winding down. Sure there were a few holdouts in the back country who came swooping down for a night attack once in a while. But "contemporary worship" held all the cities and main roads. Boomers now had their own "quality-controlled worship experience." The second revolution in worship was complete — Boomers had overthrown the (boring, dead, dry) half-mainline worship patterns of the previous generation and installed a new (more lively, upbeat) "contemporary" worship experience. Even the unsaved enjoyed this new worship product. As for worship, many pastors in their 30s and 40s now feel "we've finally got it right" — we know how to "do" worship the way we like it.

Some time ago I traveled with the youth department guys of our denomination to a series of focus groups among "twenty-something" ministers. We made no speeches, held no seminars — we just asked questions and listened. In tossing the subject of "worship" on the table one of these young pastors remarked, "Well, I've been raised on traditional worship — you know praise choruses, music projected on the wall, drama . . . that sort of thing."

Whaaaaaaaaat? *Traditional?* But of course it is true. As soon as one generation thinks it has "got it right," another revolution is due.

So, the question to think about this week is: What will the next revolution bring?

1. Have you experienced any eras of worship similar to the writer's?

2. What different worship experiences have you experienced? What were the advantages? Disadvantages?

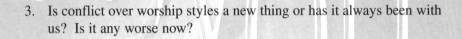

3. Is conflict over worship styles a new thing or has it always been with us? Is it any worse now?

4. What causes the most conflict in worship styles in your church?

5. How would you label the worship atmosphere in your own local church now?

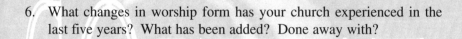
6. What changes in worship form has your church experienced in the last five years? What has been added? Done away with?

7. What changes would you prefer to happen in the next five years if you could have your own way?

8. What are the non-negotiable Bible standards of worship — that is, the things you can't tamper with or you'll be offering "strange fire" on the altar?

THE TYRANNY OF THE TELEPHONE

I hate telephone calls. In fact when a telephone rings, I actually cringe inside. Even when I hear a phone ring on TV, I shudder. I can't help it. I've always been this way. Why? I'm a preacher's kid.

When I got home from school each day, I'd look forward to my dad's arrival like it was some sort of "paternal parousia." When he came I'd get "my chance" to be with Dad. He was a good dad and gave me undivided attention at the dinner table. Except, that is, when the phone rang.

Inevitably our quiet father-son conversation would be interrupted by a harsh RIIIIING! My dad would answer it, of course. The call was often just a simple request for information (usually something he'd already printed in the worship folder or midweek mailing). Or someone might register a complaint, to which he'd listen patiently, sigh as he hung up, and return to the table a tiny bit older. Occasionally the calls signaled some sort of emergency and he'd rush off to the hospital, or over to the church. I don't remember many calls bringing good news.

Even when Dad didn't leave, he'd return to the table preoccupied. It would take five minutes to get our father-son conversation back into focus. About the time we did, another call might come. It was not uncommon for my dad to get two or three calls during dinner.

That was then. This is now. But has it gotten any better? In a pastor's home in New Brunswick a while back, I counted seven — that's *seven* — phone calls during dinner. The pastor took it in stride. But I watched his son and daughter visibly twitch as each new call came. I knew how they felt.

You'd think that with secretaries, midweek mailings and office hours, pastors would get fewer calls at home today. I don't think so. Even worse, we now have beepers! This is progress? Even a quiet walk in the park can be interrupted by a demanding beep-beep-beep. And, of course, the Devil has also brought us cellular phones! Now even the "city of refuge" status of an automobile is gone. Last fall, a pastor made four cellular calls from his van during the hour's ride back from the airport — while his ten-year-old daughter sat quietly in the back seat. Her trip to the airport was supposed to be "quality time," I suppose. (Perhaps she could have gotten his undivided attention by calling him?)

I know, I know, getting and making phone calls is "all part of the job" for preachers. Doctors get them and so do preachers — it comes with the territory. "We do it for the Lord" and all that. OK, I accept that to a degree. The pastor might cheerfully bear it, but what is it doing to the pastor's kids?

Somewhere in life a pastor has to set some boundaries, create a sanctuary where even members can't intrude — at least at the dinner table. How? I've seen several good ideas. In one home, the family flipped a switch to turn off the audible ring during dinner. Callers heard ringing, but the pastor's family didn't. (They admitted they sometimes forgot to switch it back on after dinner, however.) An increasing number of pastors "let the answering machine answer it" during supper, though others consider this deception. Where there are two lines, some ministers answer only their personal line during dinner. That seems to work, as long as the people don't catch on. I have one pastor friend who simply has an unlisted number. But his church averages over a thousand, so you might not get away with that for 100 members. Finally, I've met a few pastors who simply take the phone off the hook during supper — one is even gutsy enough to tell his people what he does.

I don't know what you do to tame the telephone, but I hope you do something — especially if you have kids. If you do nothing, be warned. Your kids could wind up like me: Every time a phone rings it will bring a shudder, a start, and a painful memory of how the telephone tyrannized your family life.

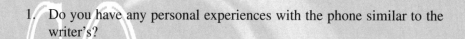

1. Do you have any personal experiences with the phone similar to the writer's?

2. Can the telephone tyrannize a layperson's home just as much as a minister's home?

3. In what ways can a church ease the burden of phone calls to a pastor's home? How many calls in an average evening at home should a pastor consider reasonable? What is a reasonable length for a normal call?

4. What are some practical hints for all of us in harnessing the phone for good use?

5. Is there anything you'd cite from the Bible or from Jesus' life which hints at putting limits on people's access to you?

6. What are some particular tips you'd suggest to your pastor in dealing with phone calls?

FIFTY REASONS WHY NEW IDEAS AROUND THIS CHURCH WON'T WORK

Somebody's always suggesting new ideas around the church, like adding on to the building, or switching Sunday school to after worship, or changing the times of services. No sooner do such ideas surface, than objections swarm up like spring mosquitoes. In order to proceed in a more orderly and organized manner, I suggest we express our reasons for why these new ideas won't work by citing the following conveniently numbered objections. For instance, "I'm against it because of 11, 26, and 44." Just think of the time we'll save!

1. It's not in the budget.
2. I need more time to think and pray about it.
3. What we're doing now is working just fine.
4. I know a church that tried it and it didn't work.
5. They never had to do that in Bible times.
6. We don't have the power to act on that.
7. Let's assign it to a study committee.

8. Some of our best givers would oppose that.
9. It's a good idea, but several years ahead of its time.
10. This sort of thing could cause a reaction.
11. It might work in California, but not here.
12. The older people would never accept it.
13. We've done OK all these years without it.
14. We can't do it until we have a new building.
15. It is too expensive.
16. It could ruin our carpet.
17. The timing's just not right.
18. Let's not be the first to try it.
19. I need to see more details before I can vote on it.
20. It's too charismatic (mainline, Mormon, etc.).
21. It doesn't fit in with our long-range plan.
22. Some of our newer people won't like it.
23. I don't see any long-term value in it.
24. That's what we hire the pastor for.
25. We'll lose people; why I know several . . .
26. It doesn't fit the culture of the people around here.
27. Good idea, but we're just not ready for it yet.
28. Our people are already overworked.
29. It doesn't jive with our mission statement.
30. That would be too radical a change at one time.
31. Our church is too small to try that.
32. Our church is too big to try that now.
33. It is a worthy goal, but quite frankly it's impossible.
34. Jesus didn't have to do that to minister effectively.
35. There are people who will stop tithing if we do it.
36. There's just not enough time.
37. In a larger city that might work.
38. Perhaps it would work in a rural area, but not here.
39. Our facilities just couldn't handle it.
40. I think all we need is to do what we're doing better.
41. It needs to be done, but we're not the ones to do it.
42. Let's let it marinate for a few months.
43. The trend right now is exactly the opposite way.
44. Everybody's not on board yet.
45. Bill Gothard teaches against it.
46. Our people are stretched too thin.
47. Our people have been asked to give too often.
48. The women's group would be against it.
49. This could be divisive.
50. We could get sued.

1. Which of these reasons is most often cited in your own church for not trying something new?

2. What other reasons which the writer omitted from the list are sometimes given for not trying something new?

3. Which of the above reasons might be cited by other churches, although you'd have to honestly say would not be a problem in your church?

4. Why does the church seem resistant to change at times?

5. What four or five things would you list to make it easier to accept change and experimentation?

6. If you were to make a "ten commandments" for introducing new ideas or other changes into a church, what would they be? How do you lead people to accept good changes?

7. What from the Bible, theology or church history suggests to you that the church has a natural inclination toward change (but resists it at first)? Why do both of these factors seem to be at work among God's people at once? Where do they come from?

STAYING ON THE CUTTING EDGE

W hy is it that some church leaders reach a zenith, then plateau or enter a period of decline? Still others, however, continue to grow and expand, staying ahead of the pack even into old age. It is true of leaders today, but it has been true throughout all history. Some leaders keep expanding, making a contribution into old age, while others make the "Great Compromise" and settle into a comfortable mediocrity. They might retain their leadership "position" but they no longer serve as true leaders. Why do some leaders fall off the cutting edge?

Seven Reasons Leaders Fall Off The Cutting Edge

1. Dream Fulfillment

Some leaders lose their punch because they finally get the leadership spot they've always wanted. They arrive, so they quit working. For ministers it may have been a lifetime goal — being elected to a certain office or getting a particular church. These leaders work like crazy while they are "on the way up," but when they get what they want they quit hustling. Several years earlier this type of leader was brimming with ideas and suggestions about "how to do it better." In fact, that's one of the reasons he got his current spot — people thought he would actually do the things he always talked about. But he didn't. What he wanted was the position of leadership, not the work. And once he had his dream job, his energies turned to holding on to the position.

Leaders who fall off the cutting edge quit pushing after they get the leadership spot they've always wanted.

Leaders who keep dreaming are leaders who last.

2. Losing Touch

By nature, leadership tends to remove the leader from the people. Leaders sense respect, admiration, even an "offishness" which creates distance between a leader and the people. Some leaders like this pedestal-ization. In fact, a few leaders actually consider it a benefit. Consider what happens to a successful pastor. Everyone asks him questions, gets his opinions, listens to what he says, invites him to speak. Before long, such a leader gets into the habit of telling . . . talking . . . speaking . . . deciding . . . declaring . . . giving opinions . . . showing everybody how . . . giving answers. Finally, this kind of leader loses the greatest tool for keeping in touch — listening. People said of one leader I knew, "I wonder why he has that hearing aid; he never listens anyway." When a leader gets stuck in the "transmit mode," he or she is soon totally out of touch with the followers. This leader no longer knows their needs, frustrations, reactions or opinions. The out-of-touch leader is the fellow who is totally shocked when he is not re-elected or appointed. It so "blindsides" him that this kind of leader will in fact probably accuse someone of politicking or underhanded political hanky-panky. He never sees it coming. Why? Because he didn't listen. He was out of touch.

Stop listening and you'll soon fall off the cutting edge.

Leaders who listen are leaders who last.

3. Stagnant Growth

Some leaders were great when they took over, but quit growing. They forgot that the standard of "greatness" keeps rising every year. These leaders were on the cutting edge once, but they coasted while their followers kept growing. Soon this kind of stagnant leader is passed by those he is supposed to be leading. The stagnant leader quits attending seminars, quits reading thought-provoking articles like this one, and quits seeking out stimulating discussions. This kind of leader eventually becomes a ceremonial leader — he shows up and plays the role. It's a sad sight to see a promising leader who was once the "best of the bunch" quit growing. Lasting leaders stay ahead of the pack by reading more, learning more, thinking more and studying more.

Stagnate and you'll fall off the cutting edge.

Leaders who keep growing are leaders who last.

4. The Fear Factor

A one word definition of leadership is "Risk." A real leader must boldly defy fear and introduce the future into the present. Like walking on water, leaders must keep their eyes on the goal, not on the threats. A fearful leader will focus on the potential political or critical consequences of new ideas and changes. He will become conservative, fearing criticism and opposition. This kind of leader looks more to the next election than to the next generation. Mediocrity is crouched at the door! The fearful leader is not really a leader at all but a mere follower of potential complainers.

Get scared of change and you'll fall off the cutting edge.

Leaders who take action in spite of their fear are leaders who last.

5. The Sheep-Recruiting Leader

One of the privileges of being a leader is to select other leaders. (In fact, it is more than a privilege — it is a major responsibility of leadership.) Though we have elections in churches, districts or conferences, universities, and denominations, the truth is that the existing leaders often influence who will comprise the next tier of leaders (and even their successors in some denominations). However, some leaders fear other potentially strong leaders near or under them. They carefully and strategically work to eliminate strong people who "cause trouble" or "ask bothersome questions." These leaders gradually populate the second level of leadership with cooperative "yes men" or women. They collect a band of dwarfs around them, imagining that in comparison they appear mighty. They don't. They look silly. "An army of lions led by a sheep will beat an army of sheep led by a lion every time. Why? Because the lion who prefers to lead sheep is no lion at all, but merely a sheep with delusions of grandeur." Leaders who refuse to recruit lions have no army at all, but are merely playing lion. Great leaders recruit strong people under them — even "lions" who oppose them at times.

Recruit weak people under you and you'll be falling off the cutting edge soon.

Leaders who recruit strong people are leaders who last.

6. Fatigue

I remember visiting one of my denomination's rising stars, who was in his late thirties. He sighed, "I'm tired . . . worn out . . . weary; I feel like a 60-year-old man." He wasn't just talking about how one feels after a hard day's work. This was an overwhelming "core fatigue." As we spoke he confided, "I'm afraid the 90-hour weeks the last several years are taking their toll." He was shell-shocked. The pace of pastoring was getting him down. Or perhaps it was the criticism he had faced. His eyes communicated a tiredness that a few days of vacation at the beach wouldn't restore. He was burning out. Such fast-rising workaholic stars shine brightly for a while, but they will be remembered eventually as the temporary flash of a falling star.

Imbalanced workaholism will knock you off the cutting edge every time.

Leaders who pace themselves are leaders who last.

7. Hidden Private Sin

Personal sin sequestered somewhere in a leader's life is a time bomb. Private sin ticks away unobtrusively as the leader rises, then finally explodes violently, leading to public disgrace and collapse. Usually. But not always. There is a second way private sin works. Sometimes it works more like cancer than dynamite. Unexposed or unconfessed private sin will eat away at a leader's confidence until the leader finally self-destructs. This sin-hiding leader makes the "Great Compromise" and settles in for a slow ride. He collects all the benefits along the way but no longer sticks his neck out, for he or she fears the bullet of exposure may be headed right between the eyes.

Hiding sin somewhere in your private life will knock you off the cutting edge.

A leader who repents of private sin and makes a commitment to live a holy life, relying on Christ's power alone, is a leader who lasts.

1. Without mentioning any names, can you describe a "great leader" who lost his or her cutting-edge sharpness?

2. Which of these reasons for losing cutting-edge leadership abilities also applies to losing the cutting edge on our spiritual life? How about family life?

3. Does God intend that all leaders remain in leadership until they die, or is it His plan that some leaders will pass off the scene before they have outlived their sharpness?

4. We are all leaders in some way and in some roles. How does the sheep-recruiting factor relate to other areas of leadership, such as family and work?

5. Can you cite scriptural examples of leaders who fell off the cutting edge?

6. What caused these biblical leaders to fall in each case?

PREPARING FOR THE EMPTY NEST

I climbed into the empty nest early. I didn't intend to; it just happened that way. I remember when I woke up and realized it. My first son was off at seminary but I still had one at home. At least he was "in the nest" technically. But it was only a technicality. If he was in the nest, I didn't see much of him around the nest very much. What I've discovered is that as soon as the youngest kid in the family gets a job and a car, the parents enter the empty–nest stage, ready or not.

The empty nest doesn't mean that your kids don't need you anymore. They still need you. They just need you when they are good and ready to need you. Which is, of course, less often than you need to be needed. And that now means that on your carefully scheduled "family days" you wind up having a day similar to that of the Maytag repairman. You sit around waiting to be needed. To schedule a father-son day, I had to compete with all kinds of other interests to get squeezed into my son's DayTimer™.

I guess I knew the empty nest was coming, but I thought it would happen much later — like when my youngest son graduated from high school, or got married, or better yet, turned 40. But it essentially happened when he got a job and a car.

It caused me to think more about the empty–nest stage of life. I've asked advice from other couples already perched in their empty nests. Many told me (with a sparkle in their eyes), "It's a great stage — you'll love it!" (Though I noticed that the husband's eyes seem to sparkle more than the wife's.) So when I was prematurely propelled into the empty nest, I asked these empty-nesters in their 50s and early 60s for advice. In general they warned me about five dangers in the empty–nest stage of life. Here is what they said:

#1 DANGER: Loneliness

Once your kids leave, your house will seem very quiet. It will be nice at first. Then gradually you'll begin feeling lonely. "No use fixing something for just the two of us," you'll say. You'll go out to eat more often. You'll ask, "I wonder what the kids are doing tonight?" You'll call them. You'll get their answering machine. You'll notice that many of the friends you made in your 30s will have gotten lost along the way during the 20 years you raised your kids. You'll start feeling lonely. It will really hit you the first Thanksgiving or Christmas you spend with only one another. You'll go out for dinner and say little to each other. You'll sit quietly watching other people in the restaurant — and think about your kids.

How to avoid this loneliness? Keep dating each other. Read a lot. Do new things. Stay interesting. Take time to carefully cultivate new adult friendships. Go back and rekindle old friendships. You'll need these friends in the empty–nest stage of life.

#2 DANGER: Gloom

You'll begin thinking more about the things you should have done with your kids. You'll think about the vacations you never took, the family days you were too busy to schedule, the promises you broke. You'll wish you'd taken more time for long walks and talks with your kids. There is so much you should have done and so much you should have told them. Most empty–nesters have these regrets. But dwelling on regrets transforms them into guilt, and finally into a deep sense of failure. Soon you'll have this "free-floating gloominess" which is so peculiar to some empty-nesters, especially men. You'll quietly brood about these missed opportunities, these could-have-beens, especially if your kids are away from the Lord. If you give in to this temptation you will eventually become a dark, brooding bore. You'll be no fun to be around, and people will start avoiding you.

How to prevent it? If you are not yet to the empty-nest stage, cash in your time now! Take that vacation you've been talking about for years. Write your family days in your calendar with ink. Put your ministry/career on hold a few years to spend more time with your kids. Take them on a canoe trip. Tour England together. Go for a hike. Visit all those professional baseball parks you've been promising yourself you'd see together. Just do it. Do it now! Few people say on their death bed, "I regret spending so much time with my kids." And, if you're already at the empty-nest stage, discard and dismiss your regrets. Don't dwell on them or permit yourself to brood. There is only one perfect Father. You aren't Him.

#3 DANGER: Materialism

You may not be rich when you reach the empty-nest stage, but you'll be richer than you were before. You'll quit buying several gallons of milk a week . . . maybe even quit buying milk in gallon jugs altogether. A cereal box will last a week! Your furniture will be bought and paid for. You'll be out of debt. And to boot, your income will probably be higher than ever. What to do? Buy new furniture — all perfectly matched? Purchase that cottage on the lake you always dreamed about when the kids were home? How about a Winnebago? Develop a fat retirement fund? Materialism is always a danger, but it is a special snare to empty-nesters.

What is the cure? Only one antidote: giving. Make up your mind now where you'll spend this "extra" money. If you don't decide beforehand, these funds will simply disappear into the thin air of either greater consumption or more hoarding for retirement. Of all age groups, empty-nesters should be the best and most generous givers to God's work.

#4 DANGER: Laziness

At about the same time your kids fly away from the nest, you may start to lose some of your own steam. Perhaps you used to stay up until midnight watching Johnny Carson. Now you start drifting off by ten — and you think Conan is a barbarian. You may begin to feel tired and weary in the afternoons. All this leads many empty-nesters to let their life fall into a comfortable half-speed routine. They are tempted to forget former obligations. You can see it with the empty-nesters in our churches who never missed a prayer meeting night or Sunday school when their kids were still around. Once their kids are gone, however, they start missing occasionally, then disappear regularly. We've all seen middle-aged couples who gave dedicated service as Sunday school teachers, club leaders and youth sponsors when their kids were active. Once the kids are gone they say, "We took our turn, let someone else do it now." Empty-nester ministers do it too. They hire more staff. They delegate more. They slow down. They cut out the "unnecessary." They start "surviving." And most empty-nest ministers volunteer less to work in their district or denomination. They prefer to sit on ruling boards and committees now, rather than take the jobs that actually require work.

The preventive? Start planning now how to spend your empty-nest time. Make a decision of the will early, then stick with it later. We ministers tell the empty-nesters in our churches to start all over again in the nursery or with the youth. We challenge them to host a small group in their home, or to begin work with children in Sunday school. But what about ministers in the empty-nest stage. How will we start over? Will we take a district "working job" instead of a "ruling job"? Will we take the equivalent of a nursery job? Will we volunteer a week at youth camp where there are no water beds? Will we launch out and plant a church? The lazy life will lead to an early grave. Decide now how you'd like to be involved. If you are already in the empty-nest stage, shock everybody and volunteer to work at youth camp or with the district CE rally. You'll be a happier person for it. God will be happier too.

#5 DANGER: Ignoring your wife

I suppose to be more correct I should say "ignoring your spouse." But that's not what I mean, really. Men need this advice more than women. The empty-nest stage grants men a pile of extra hours every week. No more evenings attending your kids' plays or soccer games. No more endless sports' banquets to sit through. (I declare, coaches are the only speakers who take longer than preachers . . . I've seen them circle the landing strip for more than an hour looking for a place to land!) No more family days cut right out of your weekend schedule. Forget that "kids' night with Dad." No more discipleship breakfasts with your kids.

The better a dad you are, the more time you'll gain when the empty-nest stage comes. It is a great gift to the man in his late 40s. He is in his prime. He has enough gray hair to look wise. He's got enough experience to avoid stupid errors. His skin has thickened enough so as to avoid getting bruised over every little criticism. He may be in the best situation since he was 18. He can look ahead the next 15 years or so . . . right down toward the finish line in his 60s. Now he has a dozen or more extra hours every week to pour into his work or hobby. So what does he do? He makes a mad dash for the finish line . . . he becomes a virtual buzz saw.

But he forgets one thing — his wife. They've been together now for 25 years or more. She is loyal. She won't leave him. She understands. She is faithful. She can be counted on. She can be taken for granted. So he pours himself into his work or hobby with a renewed vengeance. And in gaining great success, he loses his wife. She may even stay in the house with him. But he will lose her anyway.

This fifth warning came from the empty-nester wives I asked for advice when compiling this list of dangers. It was quietly whispered to me over a late-night snack when a husband slipped away for a phone call in the next room. It was also whispered across a restaurant table at dinner when a husband had wandered off to "make rounds" and greet his friends and prospects at other tables. The warning was often given with a pained look, though the woman always pointed out her own husband was not guilty of this problem.

Even when an empty-nester gains hours per week from fathering, he cannot ignore the importance of husbanding. I suppose the same thing is true of women who find time to "re-start" their careers after the kids are gone. But it is especially true for men.

1. What additional dangers of the "empty-nest period" do you observe from watching others?

2. What are the great advantages of the empty-nest period?

3. Research has shown that this stage of life brings marital satisfaction second only to the "honeymoon period." Why is this?

4. In your mind, what are the particular dangers during the "single-not-married" stage of life?

5. In your mind, what are the particular dangers during the "just-married-no-kids" stage of life?

6. How about the "pre-school/elementary-school" era of life?

7. What dangers would you cite for the retired or old-age era of life?

8. What Bible characters would you cite as good examples for the empty nest or retired era of life?

WHAT MAKES CHRISTIANS SO CRANKY?

How come Christians are so cranky lately? You know, those Christians who are prone to grumble, gripe and complain over just about everything from church music or the length of the sermon to the carpet in the nursery? Many evangelical pastors believe cranky Christians are on the increase and Christian civility is in decline. I wonder why? Do any of these prevailing theories explain it?

1. Our spit-in-your-face culture

Christians aren't exempt from our world's collapsing manners. Just a while ago I chugged to work at about 50 mph. (Hey, that's nearly top speed for my old Jeep.) I noticed an Audi jerkily following me just a few feet from my rear bumper. The driver had a "lead, follow or get out of the way" attitude. Shrugging my shoulders, I pulled partially off the road so he could pass. As the car came nearer, I noted the driver was a middle-aged woman dressed in a neat business suit. She reminded me of one of my favorite teachers in elementary school. As she whooshed past me, she caught my eye, glared at me, then summarily saluted me with an obscene gesture. Whaaaaaat? My favorite elementary-school teacher?

The truth is, we live in a spit-in-the-umpire's-face culture and we're seeing the disappearance of civility. Christians today will say or do things to their pastor that even the ungodly wouldn't have done ten years ago. The culture is rougher. So are Christians.

2. Our customer orientation

It's no secret that evangelicals have had a romance with the notion of "customer orientation." We've accepted that to be successful we must "find a need and fill it." "Do your research" and "find what they want" before designing services to meet their needs. In fact, many evangelical churches do not just have services, they *are* services. Once we start treating the attendees and prospects like "customers," they start acting like customers. And, not finding the complaint department, they tell the pastor when they're not satisfied.

3. The Freudian hydraulic

This theory says that Christians today are harried and beleaguered — under extraordinary pressure at work and home. All this stress pressurizes them like a shook-up Coke. So, when your committee discusses the comparative merits of praise choruses and hymns one evening, you pop their pull-tab and they spray all over you. Hmmmm . . . I've seen a few Cokes explode in my day.

4. Sleep deprivation

Some even hypothesize that today's Christians just aren't sleeping enough and that's why they're cranky. In 1910, before the invention of the modern light bulb, we slept about nine hours each night. Today it's about seven and a half hours. Now consistently losing an hour-and-a-half's sleep every night of one's life probably does make a fellow crabby. At least it's a nice excuse, like apologizing for your baby's crankiness with, "Oh, sorry he's so cranky; he's teething, you know." We can always say, "Oh, sorry for that outburst; he doesn't mean it — he's missed 90 minutes of sleep every night since he was born." This could explain a lot of outbursts.

5. The moral-majority boomerang

This explanation proposes that Evangelicals trained their people for twenty years on how to coerce the power structures: write letters, complain, boycott, march, circulate petitions. So (this hypothesis goes), today these same Christians have turned these same methods on their own church leadership. They write letters to ecclesiastical hierarchy, circulate petitions and withhold their tithe. Hmmmmm . . . Is there truth to this theory? Maybe, but here's one more:

6. Spiritual poverty

Are some cranky Christians simply carnal? Could the remedy be something spiritual and not just a better night's rest?

1. Many long-time pastors say there is more crankiness in the church than ever. Do you agree or disagree with them? Why?

2. How much of this crankiness is a result of our culture and how much would you attribute to spiritual problems?

3. What has changed on the part of *ministers* and *churches* in the past few decades which may contribute to the general feelings of crankiness and complaining?

4. What are your own thoughts on the lessened amount of sleep that today's generation gets compared to their grandparents? What influence does this have on marriage? Child-rearing?

5. Is there any validity to the "moral-majority boomerang" idea listed above? If so, how much and in what ways? Do you have a story or illustration?

6. Who do you recall from the Bible who was cranky or critical? What biblical insights come to your mind about the issue?

How to Get Your Denomination to Ordain Homosexuals

A 15 Step Strategy That Works

The following is a step-by-step plan for persuading your own denomination to ordain homosexuals. If you organize and follow it carefully, it will be "only a matter of time" before your own denomination ordains practicing homosexuals.

1. Make homosexuality an issue of constant discussion.

At gatherings of ministers, in your publications, at coffee breaks, and on the floor of all legislative sessions keep bringing it up. It doesn't even matter which way the discussion goes. Just bringing it up helps your cause. In any discussion or debate there is always someone who will take the "other side." This other side will agree with you, or at least be closer to you. Inflexible positions erode gradually. No position changes without discussion. The more discussion, the sooner the change. In fact, this article may even help you.

2. Recruit a prominent ally.

Try to get a prominent Evangelical to speak out for your side. Not a homosexual, but someone who will speak up *for* the homosexuals. This creates two clear positions in the evangelical church, enabling people to move a bit toward your side and look like they are on middle ground. They will say, "Well, I wouldn't go as far as Tony, but still . . ."

3. Confuse terms.

Use "homosexual" interchangeably to mean both practicing homosexual and the homosexual orientation. Don't let people know which interpretation you mean. With such confusion, church people will eventually accept terms like "gay minister" or "homosexual pastor." Initially, in publishing and speaking, this will mean ministers with a homosexual orientation. However, eventually it can come to also include people who practice homosexuality. Even Dobson uses the term "homosexual Christian." It is not that big a leap from that phrase to "gay minister" or "homosexual pastor." This confusion of terms is your doorway to change.

4. Make "gay-bashing" politically incorrect in the church.

While this term originally meant only physical attacks, it can be made to mean much more. All terms are elastic. Stretch it to encompass verbal condemnation of homosexuality. Reject "gay-bashing" in all conversations and publications — so much so that people will fear being called a gay-basher. You will know you have succeeded when your opponents begin statements on homosexuality with, "Now I don't want to be guilty of gay-bashing, but . . ."

5. Equate homosexuality with racism.

This will make people think it is only a matter of time until enlightened society moves forward, accepts homosexuality as normal and rejects our narrow-mindedness. Use the term "prejudice" often. Tell horror stories of how homosexuals are unfairly treated. If you can make this a civil-rights issue you will eventually win. There are plenty of church people who remember how wrong much of the church was on slavery and later on civil rights. By making this a civil-rights issue, you will win these people over to your side and soften their resistance.

6. Relate homosexuality to divorce.

Although divorce is condemned in the Bible, the church lets straight people get divorced — and much worse. (Sure, we do so with regret but, isn't it true that Evangelicals have come to grudgingly accept divorce as a "fact of life"?) This is a great gap in the evangelical church's defenses. Push through it. Continually argue for equal treatment of both homosexual sins and heterosexual sins. The church has gone too far. They will never turn back to again reject divorce — there are too many divorced leaders now. Eventually they will have to admit their hypocrisy and treat homosexual sinners like heterosexual sinners — accepting them both in the church, even if grudgingly. Make this connection often and loudly. It will embarrass Evangelicals and move your cause forward.

7. Steer clear of any "deliverance theology."

If the church believes that the inner nature of a person can be changed — so that the drive to commit a certain sin like homosexuality is cleansed or healed — your effort will be dead in the water. So fight any such doctrinal notion fiercely. Instead, concentrate on a "struggle theology" with emphasis on trying to "get victory" or "receive help" or be a "recovering homosexual." This will not be difficult today. It is in vogue.

8. Blame God.

Try to get homosexuals to give testimonies about how in great agony they asked God to deliver them, but He didn't. If God doesn't deliver them from their "bent to sin" in this area, how can they be personally responsible? It must be that God "made them this way." If God created homosexuals with these desires, or He won't deliver them, how can God keep them from acting on these urges?

9. Get parents of homosexuals as your allies.

Tell their stories. Get your denominational magazine to print their stories. Even the most conservative Christians become amazingly liberal where their own children are involved.

10. Work first for non-ministerial/non-membership gains.

Start first with the church's myriad of businesses and auxiliary operations. It will be much easier to get civil rights and legal protection there. Try placing homosexual employees in church-owned nursing homes, educational institutions, and day-care centers first. Then, even if these employees come out of the closet, there may be some government and legal protection. Later you can argue, "Well, you permit a homosexual to work over there, why not here in the church too?"

11. Advertise the love and devotion of homosexuals.

Remind everyone of what beautiful people homosexuals are. Keep saying, "They are created in God's image," which will imply they were created homosexual by God. Tell how homosexuals show up faithfully for choir practice, volunteer for extra work, always pay their tithe in full, and give generously to missions. This impresses Christians, and especially pastors trying to grow a church. Mention that one of the fastest growing denominations in America is the Metropolitan church, specifically for homosexuals. You will know you have succeeded when you hear a pastor say, "Well, to be quite frank, they're some of my best people."

12. Don't fight the word "sin."

Most evangelical churches now say that the homosexual orientation is not sin; only the act is sin. Their position can be summed up with, "You might be homosexual, but you don't have to act on this urge, and if you do it is sin." Don't fight this. Agree (for now) that homosexual practice is sin. Just simply equate "your" sin with "other people's sins" — like strife, greed, malice, bitterness and gossip. The secret is to not fight for homosexuality's innocence, but merely to strive for its acceptance right along with all the other sins now permitted in the church; i.e., "some gossip . . . I commit homosexual acts"; "One sin is as bad as another." The evangelical church's present doctrine of victory over sin is so weak, you'll have them in the corner.

13. Tell everyone when the first NON-practicing homosexual is ordained.

Since most Evangelicals do not condemn the homosexual orientation, but only the act, sooner or later your denomination will knowingly "ordain a homosexual" (that is, a non-practicing homosexual). Eventually someone who admits to a same-sex orientation, but who is chaste and promises to stay pure will pursue ordination. When this happens, spread the story. "We have ordained a homosexual." The more you say these words, the sooner the day will come when your denomination will ordain a practicing homosexual.

14. Get one evangelical denomination to break rank from the rest.

Eventually a fully evangelical denomination will ordain a *practicing* homosexual. Or more likely, someone already ordained will "come out." It will probably be a woman. (The church has never considered lesbianism as vile as male homosexuality.) Perhaps she will have a "life partner" on a permanent basis, which will be considered a compromise of sorts. This couple may even practice some sexual restraint or limits in their relationship. But it will happen Eventually one evangelical denomination will "break rank" on this issue — just like they once did with divorce. When this happens, spread the story everywhere. It will enable your allies to cite them as a positive example of compassion and understanding.

15. Wear them down.

Today's evangelical church has neither the patience nor the time to hold firmly to its convictions. If you stick with it, constantly arguing and gently pushing, they'll cave in. Sooner or later they will make room for homosexuals — including practicing homosexuals, even ordained practicing homosexuals — if you just keep at it.

Now, before you write hate mail to the writer of this essay, read this:

This piece is descriptive not proscriptive; that is, it was written to describe exactly what is happening in an evangelical denomination that is softening its stance on homosexual ordination. It was not written as a "how to" guide to pro-homosexual activists, but rather to *expose the strategy now in use*. The writer believes that neither practicing adulterers nor practicing homosexuals should be ordained or continue in public ministry. This chapter is an exposé of strategy to alert readers to such movements.

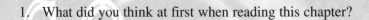

1. What did you think at first when reading this chapter?

2. Have you seen any of these strategic plans in operation in the church today?

3. Would you make any personal distinction between treatment of *practicing* homosexuals and *practicing* adulterers? Why or why not?

4. Where would you "draw the line" on including practicing homosexuals? Ordination? Lay ministry? Teaching? Membership? Attending?

5. Can a person be cured of homosexual orientation? Can God enable them to not act on it?

6. What biblical support do you have for your position on ordination and homosexuality?

THE BABY-BOOMER WORSHIP CREED

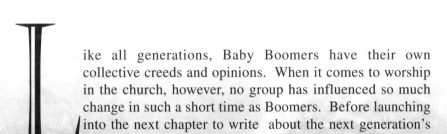

Like all generations, Baby Boomers have their own collective creeds and opinions. When it comes to worship in the church, however, no group has influenced so much change in such a short time as Boomers. Before launching into the next chapter to write about the next generation's (Generation X) worship preferences, a look at the Boomer worship creed might provide a good introduction. What do most Boomers believe about worship? If it were a creed, we'd write it something like this:

1. The Sunday morning worship hour is boss.

We recognize that some might come back Sunday evening and a few might show up on weeknights — and there are stubborn Sunday school holdouts — but frankly, we like the notion of putting on a first-class-Sunday-morning-hour-long service and letting that cover for the rest. We're too busy for much more.

2. Worship should be fast-paced.

We want worship services to crack along in a speedy format — no lagging, no dragging. That goes for time between songs, silence between people on stage, and even the speed of music. We have banned "dead air."

51

3. Good worship needs good lighting.

Some of the World War II generation gasped when we hung black pipes from the ceiling and attached our canister lights, but we knew this would enhance our services. The audience needs to see your "facials" if you expect to lead them in worship. Now we have some pretty sophisticated lighting controls, and we're better off.

4. Faith comes by hearing.

Mikes too. We chuckle at our parents' style of worship, with only one microphone attached to a wooden pulpit. We believe in mikes — lots of mikes, preferably with colorful sponges on each and (if we're really crackin'), we'll have several cordless mikes as well. The more mikes the merrier.

5. Songs should be led by a group.

We dumped the 55-year-old song leader who waved his hands at the crowd and urged them to sing louder/faster/better, and introduced our own brand of music leadership — the boomer praise team. We collected a group of Ken-and-Barbie types, practiced with them, and stuck them in front with colorful mikes. This improved our worship in most places, or at least gave us something more attractive to look at while singing. Sometimes we added an orchestra of sorts to supply even more activity on the stage to keep us involved in worship. Boomer worship has lots of thing to watch.

6. We believe worship should be upbeat.

We think the atmosphere, the music, even the preaching should be a picker-upper for hurting and stressed-out people. People who attend our worship services should feel better when they leave.

7. We prefer at least two grand performances each year.

I mean really big — something you can bring an "out and out sinner" to and be proud of — something "just as good as the world has." Christmas and Easter are our preferred times for these extravaganzas.

8. We believe in excellence.

Everything should be done first-class. We believe, "If you do worship with excellence they will beat a path to your door." Second-rate people should sing in the shower.

9. We want our preachers to be "communicators."

After all, we are the first generation raised on TV, so we expect our preachers to compete with the best communicators on the tube. The

52

greatest Boomer compliment when introducing a speaker is to call him or her "a communicator."

10. We believe singing with a screen is better than a hymnbook.

It's obvious isn't it? Hymnbooks or worship folder inserts make you look down. When looking down we can't see the praise team on stage. The screen helps us focus on the stage and God.

11. We believe recent music is better than old music.

In this we are just like our parents and every generation before them. The "old songs" they tossed out were merely the new songs earlier generations introduced when tossing out their own older songs.

12. We like to shake hands during the service.

Our parents shook hands before and after the service. We do it as part of the service. We started doing it while singing Bill's "I'm-so-glad-I'm-a-part-of-the-family-of-God." We eventually dropped the song, but still do the handshakes. We believe this creates an atmosphere of a "friendly church."

13. We like applause.

Sure, we know it tends to promote performance and direct attention to the performer, but we think it improves the atmosphere and generates excitement. It's merely the Boomer way of saying "Amen" or "Selah."

14. We don't like pulpits.

OK, maybe a Plexiglas one. But generally we prefer to see a speaker's whole body — that way the speaker can use his whole body to "communicate."

15. We think preaching should be helpful.

We like "Fourteen Tips on How to Get Along with a Difficult Person" or "Nine Ways to Overcome Adversity." We like helpful, life-related practical talks which help us survive Mondays. We even like columns such as "Fifteen Characteristics of Boomer Worship." It's just how we think.

1. The above list is a generalization and all generalizations are only partly true, so which ones would you toss out as not representing the Boomers you know?

2. If the above list were one of those *Reader's Digest* quizzes you might take to find out how much your church represents so-called "Boomer worship," how many of the 15 characteristics would be generally descriptive of your worship service?

3. What is the trouble with a uni-generation worship style? In other words, can you see any problems associated with one generation having so much influence over worship styles?

4. If these 15 characteristics generally describe "Boomer preferences" in worship styles, what would you list as the preferences of the World War II generation before the Boomers came along?

5. If you were to list four or five terms which generally describe Boomer worship, what would you list? Why?

6. What may be lacking in the Boomer worship style?

7. Does the Bible have anything at all to say about generations and worship preferences? Can you dig up any examples of worshipers' different preferences in biblical times?

GEN X WORSHIP

Boomers aren't the only generation with worship style preferences. Today's young adults, sometimes called Baby Busters or "Generation X," have their own ideas about worship. And like all younger generations, they are ready to introduce their own ideas into the traditional worship styles of their Boomer parents. Here are some generalizations about Xer worship.

1. Participation is in.

GenXers will try to eliminate performance worship. They think Boomers attract attention to themselves and not God in worship. They'll try to move worship off the "stage" to the people, and get rid of worship-you-watch.

2. Low-key atmosphere.

Xers loathe ego-oriented worship leaders and ministers. While being pleasant to their face, they make fun of "big" men who "fill up a room" upon entering. They identify big "personalities" like these as televangelist-types who are probably hiding inner moral fraud. No wonder. These moral Humpty Dumpty ministers of their lifetime have been mostly hype-types. (And they're not quite sure about the others.) What they intend to put forward are low-key, "real" people — the kind of leaders who care more about people than their own fame. During the last decade or two, low-key ministers were the bane of the church-growth types. If Xers have their way, ordinary-people-who-love may have their hey day yet.

3. "Downer" music.

Xers aren't interested in being "up" all the time. They intend to eliminate the Boomer mandate for cheery-feel-good worship, and plan to mix in more mournful, somber, "downer" music and a corresponding atmosphere and message. They think religion should be an expression of the full range of emotions, not just the happy ones. Perhaps they've been reading the Psalms.

4. Slowed pace.

GenXers don't like to gobble down their food or their worship. They like eating pizza at a laid-back, leisurely pace. That's how they want their worship too. They plan to replace the Boomer's frenzied minute-by-minute schedules with a more contemplative pace. Almost all of them speak of "silence" as a missing part of worship. [Gasp!] Ironic, isn't it? About the time the Quakers abandon silence, the Xers want to reintroduce it!

5. Out with routine!

We Boomers massacred our parents' worship routines, but merely turned around and installed our own routines. Face it, Boomer-led worship is now just as predictable as our parents' worship was. Xers intend to change all that. They want varied music, switched orders of service, a few high church elements one week, then low the next. They see no reason at all for the preaching to be in the second half of the service. They plan to mix things up each week. (Of course, they do not yet know that we Boomers intend to defend our own politically correct innovations-now-traditions to the death . . . the death of the Xer, that is.)

6. Enter: Multimedia.

Xers think illustrations should be given via big screen TV or video. They think sermons should be interspersed with video footage and interviews and not be an "endless 30-minute talking head." How will they do this without being performance-oriented? Ask them.

7. "Authentic" is trump.

Xers hate fake. They despise fake people, fake plants on the platform, fake soloists who raise their hands only when they are up front, or fake "friendship moments" when the audience is commanded to be friendly with the people around them. If it is not authentic, it is out. And the worse fakery of all is attempting to look authentic. Xers have the best malarkey meters of any generation yet. Of course, they've had plenty of malarkey to test their meters on.

8. Acceptance is mandatory.

Everything is optional to Xers in worship — except being accepting. That is mandatory. Xers plan to be wide open to all kinds of dress (and undress), styles — both old and new — hymns and choruses, overheads and hymnals, testimonies and dance, old people and children-who-cry, believers and unbelievers, women and men, black and white, Moslem and Christian. The only thing that is compulsory is "acceptance." Where'd they get this idea?

9. Relational.

Xers plan to redesign worship around a relational model. They hope to produce a more privatized relationship with God, yet a deeper horizontal F*R*I*E*N*D*S type association with others. They snicker at the Boomer handshake ritual — not because of its goal, but because of its shallowness. They think going to church with your friends is what the church *should* be. To this end they suggest planting churches for narrow slices of people — volleyball churches, Green Peace churches, backpacking churches — where the church's hobby interests are fully integrated with religion into a seamless friendship relationship. Boomers have approached church planting in a broadcast mode; Xers seem inclined toward narrow casting.

10. Outreach.

GenX wants its worship to lead somewhere. Not just to God, but to the world. To them, a worship service is more than meeting God's needs or the audience's needs — it is also about meeting the world's needs. It is outreach that isn't called outreach. Not the old door-to-door "outreach," but worship which results in things like putting on a new roof for a poor woman, taking food to a homeless shelter, or signing up to actually go to Haiti this summer, not just praying or giving. They want to do something about their religion, not just get something.

Of course all this is just generalization. And GenX folk hate it when Boomers like me make generalizations about them. In fact, they'll change their preferences just to prove the Boomer predictions untrue. Xers won't like this essay — it gives away their secrets to the older folk, the Boomers. But we can predict the Boomer response too. Now that we Boomers have installed our own worship preferences as the norm, we will say, "It's time to quit adapting worship to the people; let's focus on God — and leave things the way they are."

Perhaps that would be good. Why? Because Xers will then be forced to plant churches. And this new generation of dreamers might never do that without being forced to.

1. Who are the "Generation X" people attending your church? Name them.

2. If the above list was accurate about the Generation Xers in your area, how would the church reach this generation?

3. If Generation Xers are successful at introducing some of their changes into the present worship styles, what elements will they most likely introduce or eliminate?

4. Every generation has its sympathizers among those in the generation ahead of it. If you are a Boomer or older, which of these characteristics of Xer worship do you personally identify with?

5. Is there too much emphasis on generations in worship styles?

6. What elements of worship seem to connect with all ages?

7. If you could make one single change in the worship style and atmosphere at your church, what would you add, change or drop?

THE TRIUMPH OF ARMINIANISM

(AND ITS DANGERS)

[NOTE: This essay and the one following deal with a similar issue, the almost universal triumph of Arminian-type thinking in the practical realm of church work. They should be read together.]

Since the birth of America, the church has been mostly Calvinist while Arminianism has been a minority position. All that has changed. The evangelical church today is basically Arminian in its approach. For now, Arminianism has triumphed and Calvinism is in retreat. I don't mean that the Calvinist denominations have officially changed their doctrine. Most Calvinistic theologians have stuck with their five points. But most of the ordinary people have drifted from traditional Calvinism toward the Arminian position. The average Christian today might claim to be Calvinist, but functions as a "practical Arminian." While many Calvinist pastors still ascribe to the Calvinist shibboleths in their practical theology, they are functioning Arminians.

Arminianism has triumphed. This great theological battle was won without warfare, with few debates or "dueling magazine articles." How ironic that in a day when theology no longer matters to most people, one of the great theological battles of all times seems to have been settled. Droves of Calvinists have become Arminians — at least in practice.

Some Historical Background:

The terms "Calvinist" and "Arminian" are derived from the names of two individuals who promoted differing theological approaches. Calvinism comes from John Calvin who was a French reformer who lived in the early 1500s. He was a principal leader of the Protestant Reformation. An organized and systematic thinker with an excellent legal mind, John Calvin promoted the doctrines that eventually came to be called "Calvinism." Actually Calvinism was not a new doctrine at all. The approach was pretty similar to the theology of Augustine who lived about a thousand years earlier.

Arminianism derives from James Arminius who lived in the late 1500s. When Calvin died, Arminius was only four years old. James Arminius is not as well known in history as Calvin. But the Arminian approach was not new either. His approach was taken in the 400s and 500s by many of the early church's "Eastern fathers." One early church leader, Pelagius, even took this approach to the extreme and was ultimately condemned as a heretic by the Western church.

The Differences Between Calvinism and Arminianism

1. Does man have a role in getting saved?

A true Calvinist begins and ends his discussion of salvation with God. God alone. For the true Calvinist, man has no ability to move toward God. He cannot even recognize his own sin. Salvation is something which happens wholly as God's work. What man does or is makes no difference. Confession, repentance, or "going to the altar" does not make a difference. To the true Calvinist, salvation happens totally apart from anything man does or is. It is purely God's work done without man's participation in any way whatsoever.

Today's church has drifted to a more Arminian approach. Most church people today believe the Christian's relationship with God is "bi-lateral," not "uni-lateral." While maintaining that God alone does the saving, today's church figures that men and women have a part to play — confessing sins and receiving Christ. To today's average Christian, Christ's death on the cross provided completely for our salvation, but forgiveness is not effective until an individual receives God's forgiveness. In this most Christians are "practicing Arminians."

2. How shall we approach evangelism?

Since a Calvinist believes salvation is wholly God's work without any partnership with man, he or she approaches evangelism nonaggressively. Calvinism teaches there is nothing whatsoever a person can do to become saved — we can't "decide for Christ" or "receive Christ" enabling a person to "become a Christian." To do this would give man a part in salvation. Calvinists believe salvation is from God and God alone. To make salvation hinge on an individual's "accepting Christ" or "receiving Christ" makes salvation partially a human endeavor. A true Calvinist believes that nothing whatsoever a person does or is contributes anything at all to salvation. Salvation is God's work alone and we play no part in it — not even receiving salvation counts.

Today's evangelical church is far more Arminian in its approach to evangelism. Most Christians and even prominent Calvinistic churches emphasize our personally receiving Christ as Savior, and invite attenders to "receive Christ" or "make a decision" to become a Christian.

3. Are people totally and completely evil?

Calvinism teaches that men and woman are totally depraved — absolutely evil from birth. Every single baby coming into the world is born with an evil heart, totally depraved and completely inclined to wickedness. Total depravity teaches that men and women from birth are rotten to the core. A man or woman can do nothing whatsoever good or pleasing to God — it is impossible, for we are born absolutely and altogether sinful. Since we are born so sinfully inclined, we are therefore totally incapable of any good. Even little babies are absolutely sinful.

Most Christians today are far more Arminian. They may not use a theological term like "prevenient grace" or "common grace," but they have a hunch that God has granted some sort of grace or "light that lighteth every man" to all people on earth. In fact, even these worldlings sometimes do good things out of this positive impulse in them — an impulse planted there by God. Though this impetus is not enough to save them, it is a "God-shaped vacuum" drawing them toward God. This prevenient grace — the "grace that precedes" — enables naturally sinful men and women to seek God and to feel conviction over their sins. Most of today's Christians have a hunch that their unbelieving work associates are really hungry for God deep inside. This approach is a mostly Arminian view.

4. Did God pick who would be saved?

The Calvinist doctrine of election teaches that long before the beginning of time, God chose who would be saved. He "predestined" — set their destiny before hand — some to be saved who would go to heaven. This teaching says that out of all the people who would ever live in future history, God selected some to be saved. Some were "picked," others were not picked. The chosen ones would be the only ones saved. No one else. This view easily grows out of the conviction that man is wholly and totally depraved and unable to choose God. So, God must choose him. True Calvinists believe that God did this selection based on nothing whatsoever the individual might do or be in the future. In other words, God did not look down through history and pick those who would later choose Christ. Such a notion would make salvation based somewhat on man's later decision and not fully on God alone. Calvinists believe that God chose whom He wanted based wholly on His own criterion. Since God chose only some, those left out are destined to go to hell. There is nothing at all persons can do to escape hell if they were not chosen by God long ago. The elect are picked for salvation, no matter what they do.

Most Christians today take a far more Arminian approach to "election." They suspect that God has not limited salvation to a "select few" chosen long ago. Most people today figure God has chosen all men and women to be saved, but some reject this offered salvation and thus exclude themselves from heaven. Many today think that "according to God's foreknowledge" God elected us to salvation. That is, because He knew beforehand who would accept His salvation, He elected these ones who would later repent and receive Christ. And when it gets "real practical" — such as a baby's funeral — most folk have a strong intuition that God's grace extends to innocent babies. Few Christians today really believe that a dead baby will go to hell because it is not "on God's list."

5. For whom did Christ die?

The Calvinist doctrine of a "limited Atonement" teaches that Christ died only for a limited number of people — only for those chosen ahead of time to be saved. No one else. Calvinists believe that God chose beforehand exactly who would be saved. Thus there is no need to "waste" Christ's blood on those not chosen. Thus Christ did not die for all men and women, but only for the elect, those God picked to be saved. Christ did not die for all men.

Most Christians now believe that Christ died for all men, as a ransom for all, for the whole world. They think that any person can be saved. They are basically Arminian in this approach to the Atonement.

6. Can you keep from being saved?

The Calvinist teaching of "irresistible grace" argues that there is nothing whatsoever a man or woman can do to keep from being saved if he or she were already chosen. The grace of God is totally irresistible. Those elected by God will be saved. They can't help it and they can't resist it.

Arminians believe that Christ died for all men and thus granted common grace to all so that "whosoever will" may be saved, not just those picked beforehand. Most Christians today lean toward the Arminian approach that anyone may be saved and a person can refuse God's grace.

7. Can you quit being a Christian?

The Calvinist doctrine of the "perseverance of the saints" teaches that once you are a Christian, you are forever a Christian. Once born into God's family, you can't quit being a family member. God will never disown you. Once made alive in Christ, you can never die — "once saved, always saved." To the Calvinist, you can never divorce God from your life and He won't divorce you under any circumstance. In a word, "you can't, He won't."

While this doctrine is the best surviving Calvinist teaching, even "eternal security" is eroding from the strictly Calvinist position. Many Christians in the pew today do not believe that a person living in wicked, flagrant, open, continual and habitual sin is on his way to heaven. More likely they will say that such a person never was a Christian in the first place. And many even believe that, while it is unlikely, there is indeed a possibility that a person who was once saved could apostatize and leave God's family. While this single point of Calvinism remains, even the Calvinist doctrine of absolute unconditional security is moderating toward Arminianism.

The Triumph of Arminianism

There is little doubt about it: Arminianism has triumphed in the pew, if not in the seminary. The average Christian is a practicing Arminian, even if he claims to be a Calvinist in theory. "Practical" modern church members are increasingly rejecting traditional "five-point Calvinism." While Arminianism has been a "minority view" for decades, today there is a major shift toward Arminianism in most Calvinist churches. Why the switch?

I spent several years as a determined, "five-pointer" young man before I changed my thinking and accepted Arminianism. I made the switch purposefully and with quite a bit of painful study as a student at Princeton Seminary. But many Calvinists today are making the switch for purely pragmatic reasons. They have not become convinced the Bible really teaches the Arminian approach. Frankly, Arminianism is simply more palatable to a secular culture. It "fits in" with the mind-set of the people in their pews. Like it or not, the secular mind is naturally Arminian in its outlook. I've discovered this repeatedly myself by administering a theological questionnaire to secular students in an adult education program. These "unchurched Harrys" invariably register Arminian theologically. Face it, Arminianism is simply more logical. It makes sense to the person on the street. And today's church is scrambling to make sense to unbelievers. We want to sound sensible, logical, rational, enlightened, fair. Arminianism is so much more appealing to worldly people.

Thus, many Calvinist churches customize worship services, communication styles, architecture and music to fit the worldly customers. But they also adapt their theology by quietly creeping away from the "right end" of the theological continuum and drifting over toward Arminianism. The truth of the matter is, they are embarrassed by Calvinistic theology. They have found it offensive to the "customers." The Arminian approach to theology is simply more "seeker sensitive."

The Dangers of Arminianism

I admit that I am a committed Arminian. Of course I welcome the host of new "practical Arminians" joining ranks with my theological persuasion. I think this approach fits better with reason, tradition, experience — and the Bible. But I must be honest. There are some real hazards over here in the Arminian ocean — especially for Calvinistic churches. You can sink your theological ship here. As a local "pilot," I'd suggest you keep your eyes wide open for submerged rocks! We Arminians tend to put too much emphasis on man and his decisions, and not enough on God and the gospel. Sometimes we are tempted to act as if God is helpless without us and our work. We lean toward pragmatism and are constantly looking for "what works best," as if methodology were more important than the message. Since we believe that all men can be saved, we tend to assume that if they aren't saved, we have not packaged the invitation (or the message) right. We especially love management, leadership, programs, marketing and research data. We tend to focus more on the "potential convert" than on the eternal gospel. Arminianism easily leans toward a NIKE mentality — "Just do it." We are somewhat less inclined to pray in order to move God to "do it." And, as has always been true, Arminianism can be taken to the extreme of humanism. Calvinists have a sovereign God and an inactive man. Humanists have a sovereign man and an inactive God. Arminians lean toward the humanist end of this continuum and thus are always in danger of becoming humanists. So if you are a former Calvinist who has drifted into Arminianism with little thought and for mostly pragmatic reasons, be careful as you navigate this territory. You probably know the dangers of your former theology, especially of "hyper-Calvinism." But you may not be aware of the dangers over here. Many of us Arminians have learned to stay out of the humanist end of the spectrum. We've learned that the best place to sail is on the Arminian end, but just over the line from Calvinism.

Our five points would look something like this:

1. Total Depravity

Mankind is totally depraved, but God has extended His common grace to all so that every man or woman can search and find God.

2. Unconditional Election

Before the foundation of the world God elected all men to salvation, but most refuse His offer.

3. Limited Atonement

The Atonement of Christ is open to all men everywhere and is limited only by our refusal to be saved.

4. Irresistible Grace

The "common grace" of God is given to all men everywhere and it is irresistible, but saving grace can be refused by a stubborn heart.

5. Perseverance Of The Saints

Once saved, a person will always be saved unless by defiant, continual, purposeful rebellion he or she refuses God's grace and chooses apostasy. Though relatively rare for a truly saved person, apostasy is possible.

If you are recently coming from the Calvinistic end, be careful not to pass right by the middle ground and run off to extreme Arminianism: man-centered humanism. Instead, if you stay on the Arminian side at the end near the Calvinist line, you'll be safe in these waters. If you want a name for that area on the Arminian end (just "a hair's breadth from Calvinism"), some call this the "Wesleyan-Arminian" approach.

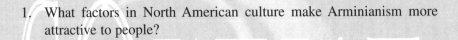

1. What factors in North American culture make Arminianism more attractive to people?

2. Of the basic "five points" of Calvinism, which one remains the strongest among church folk today?

3. The writer of this essay seems to suggest that extremism on either side is dangerous. Do you agree or disagree with this?

4. If a Christian were to hold either of the extreme positions outlined above, what could be the practical effect on this individual's daily life?

5. It is popular today to say, "We're all really saying the same thing." How do you evaluate that statement? Is it true or not?

WHERE ARE THE CALVINISTS WHEN YOU NEED 'EM?

[NOTE: This essay and the previous one deal with a similar issue, the almost universal triumph of Arminian-type thinking in the practical realm of church work. They should be read together.]

Balanced Christian doctrine is often found in the tension between two poles. That is, neither one side nor the other is completely right, but truth is found somewhere in between. Is this true of Calvinist-Arminian differences? Could it be that both views are helpful in correcting two different kinds of error? Rather than seeing Calvinists and Arminians as opponents facing each other in some sort of theological football game, perhaps we should see them as the left and right flanks of Christendom. After all, their enemy is the Enemy, not one another.

I'm not talking here about the traditional five issues we fuss about (depravity, election, limited atonement, resistibility of grace and perseverance), but rather the general approach to religion — especially as it relates to God-centeredness vs. man-centeredness. Calvinists have tended to hold down the "right side of the line," arguing for the powerful and exclusive role of God. Their religious focus is on God, not man. On the left side of the line, Arminians believe in a greater role for man/woman including a synergism with God in matters of religion.

Taking only that core issue (God-centeredness vs. man-centeredness) and applying it to the current brand of American Christianity, you've got to admit that the Arminians are in the majority. Where have all the Calvinists gone? They've gone to be Arminians. Not that denominations or seminaries have actually changed their published doctrines. What has happened is that while many Calvinists salute the Westminster confession and traditional Calvinist doctrines, they have slipped over to the Arminian side in practice. They are confessing Calvinists but "practicing Arminians." After all, how can you determine a person's (or denomination's) real theology? Your real theology is "that theology which best explains your values and behavior." Therefore, if it walks like an Arminian, quacks like an Arminian, and holds seeker-services like an Arminian, it probably really is an Arminian. At least practically.

Now, I'm not complaining about all these new converts to the left side of Christendom. After all, I'm an Arminian-Wesleyan myself, so welcome to the left side of the line . . . where we beef up man's role in religion, and give more attention to human reason, tradition and experience along with the Bible. We on the left end have been prolific in spawning movements: revivalism, campmeetings, Charismatics, seeker-centeredness, contemporary Christian music, and program-ism, huckstering all kinds of fantastic, whizz-bang programming designed to make your church successful. In fact, over here on the left is where all the action's been for the last several decades.

But I'm wondering who's holding down the right flank? The danger to American Christianity today is not becoming too God-focused, Bible-oriented, or truth-based. Rather, it is becoming a mushy, event-oriented, experienced-based, sentimental, man-centered religion. We've always counted on the Calvinist-Reformed "right end" of the line to beat back this kind of excess. But in the last 20 years, experience-based religion has been blitzing the right side of the line!

I don't mean to sound like an unappreciative Arminian. But to be quite frank, I think some of you Calvinists ought to go back over and hold down the right flank. If you don't hold down your side of the line, we'll eventually be swept off our feet and washed out to new-age humanism and universalism. Thanks for keeping us Arminians company over here on the left these last ten years or so, but perhaps you ought to go back over to the right end for a while. Don't worry, we Arminians will hold down the left while you are gone, protecting the church from absolutism, determinism, cold-hearted formalism, and too much talk about the judgment side of God. We can handle these errors, if you'll defend the faith on the right. After all, we're both on the same team, aren't we?

1. If you drew a Calvinistic-Arminian continuum, where would you place most of the people in your church on that line?

2. What excesses or error does Arminianism tend to guard against?

3. What excesses or error does Calvinism tend to prevent?

4. What are the dangers of being too man-centered in religion? Too God-centered?

5. While the writer of this essay is an Arminian, he seems to see Calvinism as fulfilling a helpful role in Christianity at large. Is this true in your way of thinking, or is Calvinism a dangerous theological error to be stomped out?

6. If you were to judge the movement of your own church the last ten years or so, would you say it is moving a bit toward the right (Calvinism) or left (Arminianism)?

7. Without getting into an argument with others, what are the chief Scriptures which support each of these positions?

BOOMER NURSING HOMES

Thousands of today's churches will become "Boomer nursing homes" in the next twenty years. These churches are jammed now with vibrant middle-aged Boomers. But soon they will become spiritual rest homes for a packed house of AARP-joining, gray-headed Boomers. Of course, the self-absorbed Boomers have barely noticed the next generation coming along, let alone been willing to listen to the changes they might want. Most Boomers will never even notice the graying of their church.

It's a funny thing how we revolutionary Boomers have so quickly become traditionalists. We have installed our kind of worship and management values about everywhere. Our generation is in charge. The World War II crowd has been beaten into submission. We are in charge. But now we've gone and become traditionalists. How'd that happen?

Easy. By establishing the reign of our own generational preferences, then simply freezing them in. We "got it right." Then we quit innovating. We quit listening. And quit changing. Many Boomers don't even know the names of the Xers in their congregations, let alone an inkling about their worship ideas. Once we Boomers installed our changes, we quickly took up defensive positions to resist all other change. After all, we Boomers know best. I know a once-revolutionary Boomer pastor who, when recently confronted with Xers' suggestions replied, "It really doesn't matter how we worship, we're no longer into changing worship styles." Yeah, sure, now that he's got what he wants!

Of course the worship music industry hasn't helped. By far the most conservative force of all, it caters to the present style of whatever is currently the politically correct music. The "now style" sells. The "next style" doesn't. Xer preferences are not even a recognized market niche. (Xers, of course, contribute to this by refusing to *become* a market niche or accepting any sort of label at all, even though they are just as predictable as Boomers.)

So these forces will combine during the next two decades to produce thousands of evangelical Boomer nursing homes. The Xers will be crowded out, marginalized, ignored. Most Boomer ministers don't even know or care what Busters want. They are tired of changing. Like old warriors, they now preach peace once they've moved in the army of occupation.

However, there will be some churches who will buck this trend. They'll reach out to Xers, gather them in, listen. And these old revolutionary-Boomers will let the Xers breathe some new life into their rigid Boomer-wineskins. Some of the changes will take us forward. Others will take us [gasp!] back. But in these churches the Xers will correct the excesses of the Boomer revolution.

But, what of the rest of the Boomers? They'll never even notice. Their congregations will age into the 50s and 60s in peace. They'll like their church. It will be pleasant there — a pleasant rest home for spiritually aging Boomers.

And the Xers not fortunate enough to find an open church? They're not very good revolutionaries, so it's unlikely they'll lead a revolution and take over the rest homes (like their parents did). More likely, they'll start their own churches. At least they'll call them "churches." Boomers won't. Boomers will dismiss their coffee houses, apartment churches, and Green Peace churches as "crazy experiments" or "nutty ideas." After all, "they don't even have a building up over there, do they?" The revolutionaries will have lost their fervor for new ideas. Few generations have lost the desire for change as fast as the Boomers.

So how about your church? Look around. Add twenty years or so to the ages of your people. What will you be then? A Boomer nursing home? Or a church who passes on the torch to the next generation? There's still time to choose.

1. If you were to make a graph or pie chart of the age groupings in your church, what would it say to you?

2. What do you think the points of contention will be among Boomers before they allow the younger generation to make changes in your church?

3. What do you think of the term "contemporary"? What is "contemporary" worship? To whom is it "contemporary"?

4. What changes do you think your own church could make to pass the torch on to the younger generation?

5. What scriptural stories come to mind that illustrate the passing on of leadership to younger generations?

IT FEELS JUST LIKE THE REAL THING!

I am embarrassed to confess what I am about to tell you. I am afraid you'll think I am lazy. Or that I am immature. But . . . but, I really like video games. I am more than a half-century old, yet I love the things. I have a few at home but those aren't the ones I really love.

The video games I really love are the brand-new, state-of-the-art editions at the video arcades in tourist areas. In fact, in airports I simply steer clear of the places, or I'll spend too much money there. That's the trouble with vacations — you have too much time and money to spend.

My favorite video game is auto racing. This last year on vacation I discovered the dream auto-racing game. First off, I got to actually climb inside this little car, with the race course wrapped around me on TV screens. If I got off the track or wrecked, the car shook and the steering wheel rattled. Every time I swerved sharply left on a banked turn the whole car tilted, just like in real life. I placed thirteenth out of the 400 players that day. (I also placed 24th — I confess, I played it a second time!)

In downtown Indianapolis there is an even better experience — a group bobsled ride. A whole bunch of us actually climbed into this little cabin with projected videotapes in front of and behind us. The whole cabin rises, falls, and jerks this way and that in perfect coordination with the videotape of the actual bobsled ride we were watching. How wonderful! The group I "rode" with came out as thrilled as if we had taken a real bobsled ride. Maybe more so!

In Canada I recently stayed in Moncton, New Brunswick at a hotel with a huge indoor game park attached. It featured fully outfitted "Virtual Reality" games complete with a virtual reality visor. This piece of head gear looks like a large motorcycle helmet, but actually includes tiny TV screens so that you can actually "see" 360 degrees around you as you turn your head this way and that. The visor/helmet places you inside the game, not outside. (I resisted the temptation to try it, but now I wish I had!)

Even home video games are moving toward VR experiences. For less than fifty dollars you can get the experience of flying a real multimillion-dollar F-15 jet airplane. You prefer submarines? For about the same amount you can have your own sub — and sail it all around the world — just like the real thing. And the CD-ROM now provides a video game with hundreds of scenarios available, just like in real life.

Eventually we will have the VR body suit. Only at the "vest" stage now, the entire suit is on its way. Similar to a diver's wet suit, it is crammed full of tiny sensors and inflating pockets which provide the sensations of whatever game you are "in." For instance, if you are having a virtual reality sword fight, the VR body suit gives you the sensation of being hit on one side or the other, perfectly conforming to the video running in your VR helmet.

So, why would someone pay hundreds of dollars for these experiences? Or for that matter, why pay one dollar to ride the auto-racing game? Here's the answer: Because virtual reality supplies all the sensations of the real thing without the risk or the cost. I can get all the sensations of racing around the Indianapolis 500 for a dollar, not a million dollars . . . and if I wreck, I won't have to go to the hospital. No risk. Low cost. High sensations. It feels like the real thing — but doesn't cost as much and involves no risk. You can have a multimillion-dollar F-15 for less than fifty dollars and fly it every evening, and if you crash, you can start the game over. Virtual reality will be successful in our culture because our culture itself is becoming a "Virtual Reality culture." We want to feel the real thing without paying the cost or taking the risk.

So, what does all this have to do with the church? Too much, I'm afraid. In a virtual reality culture, people want experiences which feel like the real thing but don't cost much or risk anything. They'll apply that to their religion too. They'll want a brand of religion which feels exactly like the old-time religion of their parents — but which is drained of most of the cost and all of the risk. This will be the "virtual religion" of the future. It will be a video arcade edition of the real thing. And it will succeed. It will succeed because it is what a virtual reality culture wants. It will succeed because this brand of religion will provide all the sensations of the real thing but without the risk or the cost. It will succeed.

But will it be the real thing?

1. What sensations of God's presence can a person feel which do not automatically mean God is actually present?

2. What costs and risks which many folk would like to avoid are part of the real religion of the Bible?

3. The writer says that virtual religion will "succeed" and be popular. What successful ministries today appear to be on the edge of this — offering the sensations of real religion without the cost and risk?

4. What influence do movies and other entertainment media, which focus so much on generating powerful *feelings,* have on what we do at church?

5. Do any of these thoughts apply to other areas of living? For example, what is "virtual marriage" or "virtual parenting"?

GOD-AS-FIRE

C hapter 19 of Acts details one of the greatest evangelistic campaigns in the early church. Starting with a core group of twelve men, Paul had in a little over two years evangelized the entire region — "all the Jews and Greeks who lived in the province of Asia heard the word of the Lord" (v.10). In addition, God did extraordinary miracles through Paul, prompting some unbelievers to seek fame and fortune by invoking the name of Jesus to drive out evil spirits. Among these were the seven sons of Sceva, who had an embarrassing encounter with a demon. Overpowering all seven of them, the demon "gave them such a beating that they ran out of the house naked and bleeding" (v.16). Quite a spectacle for the town: seven streaking evangelist wannabes!

But there was nothing at all humorous about this episode. Instead, when word spread, the entire town was seized with fear. And the believers — who? Read it — the *believers* built a bonfire. For what reason? "Many of those who believed now came and openly confessed their evil deeds. A number who had practiced sorcery brought their scrolls together and burned them publicly" (v.18-19). They had experienced the *presence* of God, but were now ready to experience his *purity.*

It was a time for fire.

The Ephesian revival teaches Evangelicals a hard truth: the Presence of God does not guarantee the purity of His people. This church had experienced the extraordinary presence of God — the entire region had been evangelized; disciples spoke in tongues, there were extraordinary miracles, so that even handkerchiefs effected healings. Even the unconverted entered the ministry to get in on the act. But the Ephesians

had kept back their "scrolls of sorcery" — a secret evil, which they had not confessed. Yet when they really experienced the "fear" of God (not just "excitement" or miracles), they quickly made a bonfire and got rid of the paraphernalia of their secret sins.

God's presence does not guarantee the purity of his people. We can have a magnificent "moving of the Spirit" in our services, yet be hiding private evil. We can lead wonderful services where people praise God, cry, and claim they sense "His Spirit as thick as a cloud," yet be collectively covering over a member's sexual abuse of little boys in the church, "because he was one of us."

We can sing wonderful hymns and choruses, with our people raising their hands. Tears streaming down their cheeks, they may even walk the aisles moved by the spirit of it all. Yet within 24 hours some of these same tearful people will be meeting each other for an ongoing secret sexual affair.

We can preach powerfully with a sense of "mighty anointing," gain great response and commitments — yet that very evening sneak off late to an adult bookstore to watch a peep show.

We can build a wonderful, fast-growing, grace-based evangelistic church in central Florida, reach more than a thousand lost people in less than a decade — yet at the same time be carrying on an affair with a woman from another state — even meeting her in a motel the Saturday night before these great Sunday services.

We can crisscross the nation, sing powerfully, lift people's spirits and turn them to the majesty of God — yet simultaneously cheat on our husband and carry on several sequential affairs with other men.

We can sob tearfully to our TV audience, boldly attack sin, the Devil, Hollywood and just about every other form of sin and debauchery — yet secretly slip off in our powder-blue Mercedes to visit a prostitute in the darkness of night.

We can build a mighty work for God, even the best "twenty-first century campmeeting" site in the nation, turn people to God — yet commit adultery with a church secretary from another state.

These are, of course, instances of *public* shame among Evangelicals. We also know there are hidden and private sins that are just as destructive. But these too seem to survive along with God's presence. The "great outpouring" of His spirit, or the "powerful anointing" on a speaker does not guarantee that the individual is a pure man or woman. In fact, God seems to "bless" some really evil people. God's presence and His purifying work may be loosely related, but His presence does not guarantee the purity of His people. What about those "lesser" sins?

We can sense that quiet hush of God's presence descending on a service — yet at the same time be guilty of materialism, embezzlement, selfish ambition and pride. We can feel God's presence so thick you can "cut it with a knife" — yet be guilty of no compassion, no burden for the lost, and a don't-care attitude toward the poor, the homeless and the unfortunate. We can feel God's anointing on our preaching, yet harbor the dark sin of racism. We can walk out of the "best service of the campmeeting," where God's presence descended like a dove, and "powerfully anointed the message" — yet within a half hour be gossiping, rumor-mongering, or telling off-color jokes at the restaurant.

We, of course, prefer for God to come like a dove, enveloping us in a sensory way so that we feel this soft, gentle alighting . . . and we sense acceptance, approval and love. Ahhhh, it feels so good.

But God also comes as fire. The other side of the "God-as-dove" coin is "God-as-fire." We seldom seek God's presence in this way. A fire does not make us feel good, or "tickle our innards." It burns. This is a sensory experience too, but it hurts — it burns, scorches us, destroys, ignites.

God-as-fire destroys sin, burns away chaff, purifies wrong motives, sets cool hearts on fire.

God-as-fire consumes the tinder of our "ministerial career." It devours habits of our old lives, singes our pride and arrogance, demolishes strongholds and pretensions set up in our hearts.

God-as-fire scorches my self-will, burns away the chaff in my hectic schedule, sends my secular values of fame/money up in smoke. Fire incinerates the private "sin compartments" we have held back from God.

Seeking God-as-dove is fine. We've gotten good at this in the last few decades, after we decided our parents had a fire-breather as God. So we ignored this side of God and invented a kinder, gentler God, one more like Mister Rogers. A God-as-dove suits our notion better. But seeking only God-as-dove gets us only half-a-God — a God who encourages, affirms, supports and admires us, but never purifies, cleanses, destroys or crucifies.

Is it not true that Evangelicals have made God a pet? He is caged up and tamed, like a fat parrot. He is no fire to fear. There is nothing about this god which creates awe. He is the sort of helper-god who finds us parking places on rainy days. I think we need to balance this view of God — with the "other side of God" — the God-as-fire.

And I'm not just talking about a passing glance at the fire, which might produce a handsome sunburn. What we really need is a face-to-face encounter with God's holiness that will give us a "first-degree burn" over 100% of the body" (of Christ).

Isn't this the side of God we sing about in "Refiner's Fire"?

Isn't it time for God-as-fire?

1. Throughout history God's people seem to swing from one extreme to the other, making Him too vengeful and angry, then remaking Him into a soft "Santa Claus in the Sky." Which extreme would you say most reflects today's church?

2. What are the dangers of either extreme (as all fire or all dove) in understanding God's nature?

3. What practical difference does holding either of these extreme views make in a person's daily life?

4. If God is *both* fire and dove (among other things like light and love), how would you explain this to those of us who cannot comprehend the seeming anomalies in God's nature?

5. If the writer is correct and today's church has downplayed the God-as-fire side, what practical steps would we need to make to restore a balanced view of God?

6. What biblical stories illustrate the God-as-fire as outlined in the last half of Hebrews, chapter 12?

7. What are the dangers of "going too far" with such a correction in our view of God?

"A" THRIVING "LITTLE" CHURCH

A while ago when I was stuck on the coast of Oregon, I attended a wonderful Presbyterian church. If the mainline church is dead, then somebody forgot to tell these people. It was a thriving congregation and I marveled at the service. As I arrived the parking lot was full, with cars jammed in all sorts of ways. I parked on the grass. Organized 149 years ago, this historic church had an unmistakable air of "permanence" — as if to say, "We've been through the Civil War, both World Wars, the Depression, Vietnam and Watergate; we'll survive anything else coming our way." Evangelical churches seldom possess this sense of permanence.

Inside, the worship atmosphere was charged with expectation and meaning. I wasn't sure where this was going, and then the music started. The singing was led by a thirty-five-ish woman who sprouted spiked jet-black hair that leapt from her head like an erupting volcano. I figured she probably belonged to the Sierra Club, ate granola and displayed a "Save the Whales" bumper sticker on her Volvo. I groaned. But, she got the people singing. It sounded like a thousand voices filling the church. She scolded the people a bit for "wanting only familiar Christmas songs," and warned that they'd be singing mostly old songs, not "the popular songs of the last 100 years." (?!)

Speaking of hymns, we sang five full hymns, two before the sermon and three after — none of them back to back. People sang heartily, accompanied by what looked like a hundred-year-old organ (played by a lady only a bit younger). The music "filled" the room, encouraging me to sing louder myself.

The Boomerish pastor was shiny-bald on top, but compensated with a bonus crop of hair around the edges and over his ears. He had earned a doctorate from some university in Germany I can neither pronounce nor spell. His message was about the only source of hope for today: the Word of God. The order of service reflected that focus, featuring a long Old Testament reading, a responsive Psalm, a New Testament reading, plus a lengthy gospel reading. (I wonder why evangelical churches who prattle the most about the authority of Scripture act the least like it really is important to a worship service?)

Right before the offering, the pastor came down among the people and asked for prayer requests. This was a kind of testimony time and among concerns expressed were the physical needs of the people and the homeless shelter sponsored by the church. The pastor then prayed at a leisurely pace — for several minutes — with great pauses between sentences, as if he expected us to fill in the dead space with our own prayers. The sacrament of Holy Communion was served, with four women distributing the elements.

The service lasted exactly one hour. This amazed me. They seemed to do so much in an hour, yet were not rushed. Following the service we were all invited to the back of the sanctuary for coffee and heaps of homemade cookies and tiny little sandwiches.

I liked the service. I liked the people. There was a thriving atmosphere, as if they knew what they were about and where they were going. If I were to move into the community and look for a church, I'd sure consider this one.

But what most shocked me was their size. About halfway through the service I counted (I confess, I'm a recovering Boomer!) fifty-two people. I counted again. Sure enough, fifty-two. The actual church building only measured 24' X 24' with an "addition" of about the same size (I checked the drywall seams). There were only twelve pews. Each looked crammed if it boasted five people. More than twenty people sat in chairs set up along the edges, which gave an "overflow crowd" feel to the service. The cream-painted walls were set off with sparkling white wood trim. There was a single window facing south — a simple stained glass one.

What haunted me as I left — no, it outright irritated me — is how this little church of 52 could seem so successful . . . so thriving. Didn't they know they were considered a failure among the church-growth gurus? What right did they have to act so happy, so joyful, so satisfied with their little dinky church of 52? A church of 52 isn't viable — haven't they read the same books I have? And another thing, why would a guy with an earned doctorate from a prestigious German university be so happy pastoring 52 people? Where'd he get his notions of success? Didn't he know that he'd never be invited to speak at a ministers' conference to tell others how he did it? Why would he waste his life away in a church of 52? What was going on here?

I left church that Sunday wondering what these people had that most evangelical churches have lost. Evangelicals are always reaching for the goal of success. Always striving, never thriving. This sense of thriving always seems just around the corner . . . when we reach 100, or 300, or 1000, or after we get our new building. But it is seldom a present-tense experience. Like drinking seawater, we can't get enough and the more we drink, the thirstier we get. Yet this little Presbyterian church of fifty-two seemed to focus more on *being* the church, than *growing* the church. I can't get that little congregation out of my mind. They have something to teach us all. What gives this sense of thriving to a church? What can we learn from them?

1. In what ways is an atmosphere of success or a feeling of "thriving" related to numbers? To mind-set? To expectations?

2. What factors during the last ten or so years have made so many churches feel like they are failures or that they are too small?

3. What practical steps can a smaller church take to capture this sense of "thriving" despite being smaller?

4. Even though giant churches get all the attention, the majority of churches of all denominations in America are well under 100 in average attendance each week. Why do these churches survive? Why do people attend churches with attendance under 100?

5. What actual advantages of smaller churches are often overlooked in our quest for church growth?

6. Is there such a thing as an "optimum size" for a Christian church — the size where it functions best? Is the optimum always bigger?

7. What connections do you make between the church and cultural factors like shopping malls, auto-superstores, mini-malls, boutiques, or 7-11 stores?

15 CHARACTERISTICS OF GENERATION X

I spend a month or two every summer hiking on the Appalachian Trail with hundreds of Generation Xers. I hike incognito, never telling them I am a minister or college professor. They usually don't ask anyway. For me, it is not a trip to witness to them so much as to discover what the younger generation is really like — without their barriers up. Thus, I get a pretty good glimpse of the secular Xer. They are a fascinating generation, quite different from their Boomer parents. The characteristics I've discovered about Generation X on these hikes are:

1. Higher view of marriage.

Burned by their parent's selfish divorces, they intend to marry for life, and thus have a higher view of marriage than the previous generation. They will wait for the "right one" — even for a decade. As one 21-year-old chemist put it, "For me it's one life/one marriage."

2. Lower view of sex.

However, their view of sex is lower and largely disconnected from marriage. Living together before marriage, or having safe sex with somebody you like is accepted almost as much as my generation accepted "making out" before the wedding night. One female medical student put it this way: Sex is like playing tennis — something you do for fun with somebody you like and has nothing to do with marriage."

3. Selectively high morality.

One 17-year-old hiker, who was picking up food in town, got soaked by the rain. A pretty twenty-something woman remarked, "You look like you could use a shower." He could, he said, and she took him to her apartment for the night. Apparently worried about statutory liability, she asked him point-blank, "How old are you?" When he caught up to me the next day and told the story he said, "Well, I couldn't lie to her, of course . . . so I wound up sleeping on the couch." This Xer was quite willing to *sleep* with this gal, but he wouldn't *lie* to her.

4. Tolerant.

GenX accepts just about everything except narrow-mindedness. They have absolutely zero tolerance for intolerance. To even appear so brings shunning, scorn and rejection.

5. Spiritual.

They openly explore their spiritual sides. Terms like spiritual, healing and soul are all common.

6. Universalist.

While they are spiritually oriented, their interest is much broader than the One God of the Bible, and includes Buddhism, Hinduism, and all kinds of New Age philosophy mixed in with remnants of Christianity.

7. Biblically ignorant.

They know next to nothing about the Bible. Out of one group of 15 Xers, not a single one knew the story of Abraham offering up Isaac. When they heard it, though, they approved it and thoughtfully pondered its meaning. One said, "I went to church every week as a kid; how come they never told me that story?"

8. Experiential.

Their surety comes from experience, not objective truth. One 31-year-old philosophy grad nicknamed "Slider," who now works as a cook, claimed he was an agnostic. This was based largely on his negative experience with a fundamentalist church in Texas. He joined me on the top of a thousand-foot cliff to watch the sun sink softly one night. Moved by the grandeur of it all he burst out, "There's got to be a God . . . there's just got to be!" Personal experience had determined his view in both cases.

9. Doubt without guilt.

A guilt-relieving approach to evangelism doesn't cut it. These Xers don't feel like sinners, even though they suspect the church thinks they are. Instead of guilt, doubt is the issue; instead of forgiveness, faith.

10. Beer is boss.

Off-label beer especially. I saw only one instance of drunkenness, but off-label beer was everywhere. Not only would they walk five miles into town for a beer, but these hikers would add a half-dozen bottles to their 40-pound packs, and haul them ten miles to a campsite just to share with others. (They sometimes brought me a Coke, assuming that a teetotaler like me was probably a "recovering alcoholic.")

11. Non-workaholic.

They aren't non-alcoholic, but they are non-workaholic. These children of climb-the-ladder Boomers figure a job is what you do to earn money in order to live. It is a means, not the end. One conversation reflected this value best: "Why do you choose to only work four days a week?" Answer: "Because they didn't make three days available."

12. They believe they're OK eternally.

They think they'll get to heaven, if there is one; that God will be more broad-minded and accepting than most church people are. They really have little fear of judgment, hell or eternal punishment, and doubt that "God would do such a thing."

13. Relational.

They are good friends and value friendships. They're hungry for someone who will take time to listen, relate in a low-key way, and avoid being preachy. Their complaint about their Boomer parents: "They never took time for me." They thirst for friendships with people their parents' age.

14. They dismiss "organized religion."

Generally speaking, they consider "organized" religion to be narrow-minded, hypocritical, money-grabbing, intolerant and irrelevant. They much prefer their own brand of do-it-yourself syncretism.

15. They consider "evangelism" obnoxious.

Most have had a personal experience with being evangelized somewhere along the line . . . and it was bad. They are open to friendship, but closed to (overt) evangelism.

The question, of course, is how does the church reach this generation?

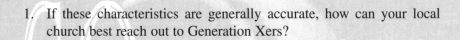

1. If these characteristics are generally accurate, how can your local church best reach out to Generation Xers?

2. What evangelistic formats may not work like they once did?

3. What new evangelistic formats might work better with this generation?

4. How can the church deal with this generation's tendency to refuse exclusivity; that is, their rejection of the claim that Jesus is the *only* way to God?

5. Who are the secular-unchurched Generation Xers you know? Who are the churched Xers you know? Where would the unchurched make their first positive contact with your church?

THE HOLINESS MOVEMENT IS DEAD

[NOTE: This essay was first given as a jolting address to the presidential luncheon of the "Christian Holiness Association" and was later reprinted elsewhere. Though it is an "insider" address that applies primarily to the denominations in the so-called "holiness movement" (of which my own denomination is a part), some of these observations may apply to all evangelical churches. If this writer is correct in his other estimates, the "evangelical movement" and the "charismatic movement" (perhaps all movements?) are soon to be in a similar position.]

I owe a lot to the holiness movement. In 1905 or 1906, my grandfather, an immigrant coal miner, came from England to the United States and settled in Pennsylvania. At the Five and Dime store, his wife Emmaline met a woman who seemed different. The woman asked my grandmother, "Would you like to come to a cottage prayer meeting?" Emmaline had attended the Church of England all her life but, since coming to America, was not attending a church anywhere. She said, "Why, sure!" And my grandmother, Emmaline Drury, got into a small cottage prayer meeting of the holiness movement. In it she found the Lord — she got "saved." She didn't even know what saved meant, but she got it.

She came home to my grandfather, Walter Drury, and told him, "Walter, I got saved tonight." My grandfather said, "Well, that's fine Emmaline." (But to himself he said, "We'll see.") Up to that point he had always come home from the mine and gone into the basement of that home in Elizabeth, Pennsylvania to take off his working clothes. The very next day when he came home from the mine, he walked right through her kitchen, upstairs to the bedroom, took all his filthy, coal-black mining clothes off and plopped them on the bed. Emmaline followed him upstairs and without a word, picked it all up, cleaned up the bed, took everything outside and shook out the dirt. He did this every day for two weeks! She smiled, never said a word, and with a sweetness of spirit cleaned up after him every day. This was salvation, folks, not sanctification! My grandfather was so affected by her response that he went with her to the cottage prayer meeting. He too was saved in a holiness meeting in Elizabeth, Pennsylvania.

So, I owe a lot to the holiness movement. My grandparents raised my father, who became a holiness preacher. And now I follow in that path.

However, what I have to say is not a collection of bright and cheery thoughts. It is this: We need to admit to each other that the holiness movement is dead. We have never had a funeral and we still have the body upstairs in bed. In fact, we still keep it dressed up and even talk about the movement as if it were alive. But the holiness movement as a movement is dead. Yes, I recognize that there are many wonderful holiness people around. And people are still getting entirely sanctified here and there. But as a movement, I think we need to admit we are dead. The sooner we admit it, the better off we'll be.

We have a holiness heritage. We have holiness denominations. We have holiness organizations. We have holiness doctrines. We even have holiness colleges, but we no longer have a holiness movement. I, for one, lament the death of the holiness movement. But pretending we are alive as a movement will not make it so. In fact, it may be the greatest barrier to the emergence of a new holiness movement.

What happened to the holiness movement? How did the movement die? Who killed it? Was it a slow death, or did it die suddenly? Was it murder? Suicide? Why did the movement die? What caused its death? I wish to suggest eight factors which contributed to the death of the holiness movement.

1. We wanted to be respectable.

Holiness people got tired of being different and looked upon as "holy rollers." Somewhere along the line we decided we didn't want to be weird. We no longer wanted to be thought of as a "sect" or a fringe group. Instead, we wanted to be accepted as normal, regular Christians.

We shuddered at the thought of being a "peculiar people." We determined to fit in.

Pastors in holiness churches now tell visiting speakers, "My people here are quality people." What they mean by "quality people" is that their church is populated with sharp, upscale, white-collar professionals. "Quality people." Respectable people. And we have become respectable. There is not a whole lot that distinguishes us now from other Christians. Presbyterians, Baptists and Lutherans move into our churches from their former denominations with ease. They don't see that much difference, because there isn't much difference. We have succeeded in becoming average Christians.

But in our quest for respectability, we lost something. We lost our willingness to be "different." Not just different from the world — but different from average Christianity. We left the fringe, we became respectable, and somewhere along the line we lost the movement.

It is hard to be a holiness movement when we don't want to be different from the average Christian.

2. We have plunged into the evangelical mainstream.

Over time we quit calling ourselves "holiness people" or "holiness churches" or "holiness colleges" or "holiness denominations," (except, of course, to each other). We began to introduce ourselves as "Evangelicals." We started becoming more at home with NAE than CHA. Local churches repositioned themselves as "evangelical" in their communities. We built respectable churches on busy highways. We quit painting "Holiness unto the Lord" on the front wall. And gradually we were assimilated into the evangelical mainstream.

All this, of course, was quite easy for us. Mainstream evangelical media kings like James Dobson, Charles Colson, Pat Robertson, Jerry Falwell, Robert Schuller and Bill Hybels melted away our differences. Few holiness kingpins are to be found. And even those who have a holiness background are not so much known as holiness leaders as evangelical leaders. The influencers of our pastors are Evangelicals, not holiness leaders. Gradually the theology among our people became the same generic evangelical soup served at any other evangelical church. "Holiness people" became "evangelical people."

It's hard to have a holiness movement when our people are really a part of the evangelical movement, not the holiness movement.

3. We failed to convince the younger generation.

We must admit to each other that we have generally failed to convince the generation in their 30s and 40s of the importance of entire sanctification. A few preach it regularly. But many preach it only occasionally, and even then with little urgency or passion. It is not the "primary issue" for Boomer and Buster preachers. At best, holiness is preached as an attractive accessory, not as an essential necessity. This generation (my own) made it through the ordination hoops, then put holiness on the back burner.

Many grass-roots people like to blame the educational institutions for this, of course. But all of us must shoulder the blame. We need to face the music. Many holiness pastors have opted for the much more appealing notion of optional or progressive sanctification than for such a notion as "instantaneous," and/or "entire" sanctification.

It's hard to be a holiness movement when many of the aggressive Boomer and Buster pastors do not preach holiness, and if they do, do it with little passion or insistence.

4. We quit making holiness the main issue.

In the movement stage "the main thing is to keep the main thing the main thing." When the holiness movement was a movement, holiness was the main thing. Holiness was all ten of the top ten priorities. Everything else was brought into line behind holiness.

Other movements illustrate this. Consider the anti-abortion movement. There is little room for anything else. Fighting abortion is the main thing. All actions are brought under this issue. All judgments of people and organizations are made through the glasses of the "main thing." Or consider the church-growth movement. Here, growth is the main thing. Will it help us grow? Will it hinder growth? These are the questions when a movement is a movement. The dominating priority relegates all other matters to secondary priorities. This is one of the excesses of a movement. The term "balanced movement" is an oxymoron. Movements are radical by nature.

There aren't a lot of excesses in the holiness movement today. We're pretty safe. Holiness is our stated belief. But in most places we don't make it the main thing. Preachers in the old holiness movement used to say, "Preach holiness and everything else will take care of itself." Who says this today? Today's trend is uplifting, cheery, help-for-Monday sermons, not holiness sermons. When holiness is not the main thing there will be no holiness movement — just as whenever abortion is not the main thing, there will be no anti-abortion movement.

It's hard to have a holiness movement when holiness is no longer the main thing.

5. We lost the lay people.

A real movement is not made up of professionals but is lay-dominated. While holiness preachers and writers ignited and led the laymen in the old holiness movement, the laymen provided the real dynamic. But over the years, gatherings of the holiness movement like CHA have become fellowships of ministers on expense accounts, not a crowd of laymen with a personal passion for holiness. In fact, one wonders how many meetings we would have if all those who attended were paying their own way. We no longer have a force of lay foot soldiers. We have generals without armies — strategy, but no soldiers.

It's hard to have a holiness movement without the laymen.

6. We overreacted against the abuses of the past.

I am not yearning for the past. I believe the holiness movement, in many cases, had an abusive past. But in trying to correct these abuses, we overreacted. Some (perhaps most) in the old holiness movement were legalistic and judgmental. So we became behavioral libertarians. Some were so ingrown as to never touch the world. So we became assimilated into the world and seldom touched God. Some were radically emotional, running the aisles, shouting, and "getting blessed." So we became orderly and respectable, and we labeled all such emotion as "leaning charismatic." Some were judgmental and rejected anyone who got divorced or had marriage problems. We became so accepting of divorce that it is quickly becoming a non-issue for all but the clergy — and even that is eroding. They preached a fearsome, vengeful God. Now we have a soft, easygoing Mister Rogers in the sky, "who loves you just the way you are."

While the abuses of the old holiness movement were glaring (and perhaps responsible in part for our own overreaction), the abuses of our own generation have been no better. We have led many holiness folk far from essential holiness doctrine and experience. We now have holiness theologians and speakers (like myself) who are better at articulating what holiness is not, than what it is.

It's hard to have a holiness movement when much of what we are is merely a reaction against who we were.

7. We adopted church-growth thinking without theological thinking.

We discovered that in America numerical success is the doorway to respect. We wanted to be accepted into the mainstream and we found that church growth gave us the chance. When the church-growth movement first came along, holiness people were wary. We were nervous about too much accommodation to the world in order to win the world. But evangelism has always been a twin passion with holiness. Thus, many holiness churches — at least the growing ones — suppressed their natural reticence and adopted church-growth thinking in a wholesale way.

Pastors became CEOs. Ministers became managers. Shepherds promoted themselves to ranchers. Sermons became talks. Sinners were renamed "seekers." "Twelve steps" became the new way to get deliverance. Growth itself became the great tie-breaking issue. Everything else was made to serve growth.

Of course, there is nothing wrong with church growth. And if people are getting saved, there *should* be church growth. But is there anyone who would argue that the church-growth movement is in any sense a holiness movement? In fact, much of the movement is quite openly anti-holiness, instructing us that "perfecting the saints" is an unfinishable task which should be given secondary importance to the primary task of initial disciple-making. Most of us in the holiness movement (myself included) joined the church-growth movement with great gusto. And with little theological thought. (I might add that this transfer of loyalties from the holiness movement to the church-growth movement was encouraged by most holiness denominational leaders like myself. And we leaders restructured all the denominational reward and affirmation systems to encourage only two things: growth and "bigness.") And we got what the denomination rewarded — at least for a while.

Holiness pastors became enthusiastic foot soldiers in the expanding church-growth movement — which was indeed a movement. They read church-growth books, attended church-growth conferences, subscribed to church-growth magazines, and networked with other like-minded church-growth pastors. This is the stuff of a "movement." These holiness pastors had simply switched movements. They traded in the rusting, old holiness movement for a bright, shiny new church-growth movement.

(As a side point one wonders, now that the church-growth movement is crumbling, where these pastors will go next. Presumably, the church-growth movement will continue to produce publications, hold conferences and grant "D. Min" degrees in church growth for many years. And I suppose that sooner or later someone in that movement will speak to a gathering of church-growth thinkers and pronounce the movement dead.)

Many holiness pastors just switched movements. They became members of a bigger, stronger, more popular and better financed movement. Can anyone deny this? In many holiness churches growth is king, not holiness. Pastor and people are in the church-growth movement. And because of the radical nature of a true movement, it is difficult to ride two horses at once. So we ride the church-growth horse and have turned the holiness horse out to pasture.

It's hard to have a holiness movement when our hearts have already been given away to another lover . . . another movement . . . the church-growth movement.

8. We did not notice when the battle line moved.

Many of us believe we are in danger of losing the doctrine and experience of "second-blessing holiness" — an experience through the Holy Ghost which cleanses the heart of its inclination to rebel and enables the believer to live above intentional sin, producing a life in obedience to the known will of God.

We believe that we should stand our ground for the holiness message — that holiness is the "front line" of battle, if we use military terms. But while we have been meeting and talking to each other about holiness, and while we have been discussing doctrine in the Wesleyan Theological Society, and while we have been having our denominational conventions where we show each other our self-congratulatory videos, the battle line moved on us.

Many of our people do not need to be sanctified — they need to be saved! The doctrine at risk in many holiness churches is not entire sanctification but "transformational conversion." We may need to stand at Luther's side a while before we can rejoin Wesley.

Few will admit it knowingly, but many of our churches have replaced "transformational conversion" with a softer, more user-friendly style of building the local church. "Membership assimilation" or "assimilation evangelism" or "faith development" models seem so much more attractive today than the old sin-repentance-conversion-restitution models of the past. The notion that people can repent of their sins in a single moment and be transformed instantaneously into new creatures with radically changed lives is increasingly at risk, even in holiness churches. Modernity teaches us that nothing can be done in less than twelve steps!

These popular assimilation models turn the gospel into something else. It is more sociology than theology. People ooze into churches without ever becoming saved. Repentance is replaced by "accepting Christ." Christ is "added on" to achieve a balanced life. Sinner is traded in for "seeker," absolutes for options, and theology for therapy.

And people do come into the church. And growth — even great growth — results from these "nonconversion" conversion models of church growth.

But it is hard to have a holiness movement dedicated to the possibility of "instantaneous sanctification," when many folk do not even have an experience of "instantaneous salvation."

It's hard to have a holiness movement when many of our own church members are not even saved, let alone sanctified.

My sense is that, as a movement, we are dead. And the sooner we admit it, the better off we'll be. While the doctrine and experience of holiness still has more life than the movement, my sense is that these too will follow the movement in death. And if I am correct — even half-correct — holiness people are at a critical point in their history.

But here is the irony in all this: There has seldom been a time when the church more desperately needs the holiness message. Spiritual shallowness is rampant. Sin among believers is commonplace. Christians boldly advertise on their bumper stickers, "I'm not perfect — just forgiven." What was once an eroding morality in the world is now an eroding morality in the church. People like Peggy Campolo call themselves "evangelical," yet they "enthusiastically endorse . . . monogamous, loving, intimate relationships between people of the same sex." Evangelical?

The church watched Amy Grant and Michael W. Smith succeed in becoming crossover artists . . . and then followed them with crossover worship services. We were delighted that our music, support groups and encouraging talks were popular with the world. We started to fit in. The world liked us! Christians are less and less different than their unsaved neighbors. They are out for the same thing. They lie, cheat and get divorced just like their unsaved neighbors. The old riddle was prophetic: What's the difference between the church and the world? Answer: About ten years. Perhaps even less.

Evangelicals have accommodated divorce. "Worldliness" is seldom mentioned, and even then only in jest. Evangelicals now attend the same movies as the world does. They rent the same videos. They watch the same TV shows. Evangelicals watch things on television which they would have called "pornography" twenty years ago. Christian families are falling apart. Even sets of board members get divorced and marry each others' spouses — all while staying on the board! And evangelical churches are filling up with people who have never had a genuine experience of transformational conversion. They ooze in through the sociological assimilation process.

Isn't it ironic that just as the holiness movement enters its waning years, the church-at-large has its greatest need for a holiness movement? What does God want? I believe He wants a holiness movement. A new holiness movement . . .

> . . . a movement which will boldly preach that God is holy and does not accept sin.
> . . . a movement which will have the integrity to tell some Christians they need to get saved.
> . . . a movement which will preach a second work of grace which God does in the life of a believer to cleanse and empower him or her, enabling that believer to have an obedient life of devotion to God.
> . . . a movement which will call people to abandon worldliness

— even at the risk of losing some people to the positive, upbeat, cheery service offered down the street.

. . . a movement which will adopt an external mission — to recruit, persuade and mobilize other Evangelicals as aggressively as the church-growth movement or the anti-abortion movements have done — to recruit them to holiness.

This is the holiness movement today's church so desperately needs. A new holiness movement.

So, my outlook is not essentially gloomy. True, for the holiness movement of the past decade or two, I am pessimistic. But for the new holiness movement of the next decade or two, I am quite optimistic. I believe we will see it! God will bring it!

The disturbing question is this: Will the old holiness movement be in the new holiness movement? Will God go outside our circle to raise up someone else to lead the new movement?

I think it would be wonderful if God would raise up a new holiness movement within the holiness movement. Maybe we will admit that the holiness movement is dead. And we will organize as a "remnant" within the holiness movement. We will become more like an underground movement than an official movement. A holiness movement within the holiness movement. Perhaps we could become the "holiness good news" movement within the holiness denominations. We could be it. But I fear it will not be. God is often forced to use new wineskins to carry His new wine. We may care more for our old wineskins — camp-meeting, revival meetings, holiness conventions and the like — than we care for the new wine.

However, my proposition may be totally wrong. Maybe God will raise up the old holiness movement to be the new one. Perhaps I have painted too bleak a picture. Perhaps I am too much like one of the mourners at the funeral of Jairus' daughter . . . I lament her obvious death. She's pale. She is dead. She's gone. But Jesus is standing nearby. And He will say, "She is not dead, but asleep." I will laugh! But He will take our movement by the hand . . . and speak to us: "My child, GET UP!" And a new holiness movement will arise out of the old one.

Whatever He does — by birth, renewal or resurrection — when the new holiness movement comes along . . . I want to be in that number!

1. What is your own recollection of the "holiness movement" (or any other movement you are familiar with)?

2. What are the factors which lead to the birth and death of movements in Christianity?

3. The writer has painted a pretty bleak picture of the holiness movement. At what points is he accurate in your opinion? Where does he seem to be stretching it?

4. As you examine the Christian scene today, what would you say is the predominant movement? Why did this movement come into existence?

5. What role do you believe God plays in the birth and death of movements within His church?

6. While a "holiness movement" may die away, holiness itself cannot pass away, for it is rooted in God's Word. Where do you see the call to holy living, to the surrendered life, to absolute commitment coming from today?

CHRISTIAN SECURITY

C an a Christian stop being a Christian? Would God disown one of His own children? Did Judas go to heaven? Once you are saved are you always saved? There are two general views here.

Unconditional Security

This view is that once you are saved you are always saved — nothing can ever end your relationship with God. The extreme view of unconditional security runs something like this:

"When I become a Christian I am adopted into the family of God based on Christ's death, and not on anything whatsoever that I have done. I can't save myself, only God can do this. When I was saved I was born into God's family. I did nothing to birth myself — God did it all. And I can do nothing to keep from being a son or daughter — I have that right by birth, not behavior. There is nothing I can do which will make me quit being a son or daughter. Nothing whatsoever that I can do can separate me from God's love. I am a child of God by birth. True, I might get out of fellowship with God. I might even wander off into the far country like the prodigal son did. But even in a distant land of disobedience, I am still a son — just a son out of fellowship with the Father. My relationship with God is fixed for all eternity, and even if I spit in the face of God I will still be His son. Once a son always a son. Let's say I become a Christian as a teen, drop out of all religious things for thirty years, live a life full of sin, then decide to get right with God again. This unconditional security group will call this a 'recommitment' not salvation, since they believe I was a Christian all that time, just 'out of fellowship.'"

To those who believe in unconditional security, nothing can make a Christian lose his salvation. If a little boy prays to receive Christ in a Good News Club at eight years of age, he is permanently grafted into God's family. This sonship is permanent and unalterable no matter what he does from then on. If that little boy grows up to live a life full of drunkenness, drugs, immorality, rape and murder, he still goes to heaven. His salvation is not based at all on anything he did or does — but totally on what God did for him on the cross. This is the radical view of unconditional security. When a person is justified it is once for all. All the convert's sins — past, present, and future — are forgiven. So future sins are irrelevant to his salvation — they have all been forgiven in advance 2000 years ago. As far as his salvation goes, sin is irrelevant.

People on this side of the road don't need to worry much about sin in their lives. They can simply rejoice that "There is therefore now no condemnation for those in Christ Jesus" (Romans 8:1 RSV). Being in Christ is irrevocable insurance — the premiums were all paid in advance by Jesus' death.

In its most radical forms, unconditional-security proponents will argue that if the Lord returned today there would be thousands of people raptured right out of the arms of prostitutes or gay lovers, for their salvation is not based at all on any behavior, but only on something which happened in the courts of heaven.

This radical form of unconditional security follows the far left side of the road. But there is a path on the far right side, too.

Eternal Insecurity

These folk steer to the other side of the road, constantly anxious about their own salvation. They disbelieve unconditional security so much that they practice eternal insecurity. They believe "one sin and you're out" of God's family. This sort of insecurity leads to spiritual hypochondria as people constantly check their pulse to see if they're still spiritually alive.

If these eternally insecure people slip into sin, they feel they have to get born again . . . and again . . . and again . . . and again. One single slip is grounds for expulsion from God's family. Any thought, word or deed which is disobedient breaks the relationship with God and will damn the individual.

People on this insecurity path are never sure. They are not sure if they are in or out today, so they turn morbidly introspective trying to eliminate any vestige of wrong thoughts, words or deeds. They reason if they live a perfect life — totally free from any sin — that then they will be saved.

They mistakenly focus on themselves instead of Jesus, as if all responsibility for staying saved is theirs and God is somehow looking for an opportunity to kick them out of the family. In their preoccupation with human effort, they are more humanist than Christian.

Both sides of the road are extremes: those who argue for unconditional security, and those who are eternally insecure about their salvation.

Is There a Middle Ground?

Perhaps. Try these thoughts for starters . . .

1. God's love is unconditional.

There is nothing that can separate us from God's love. In fact, God's love was extended to us while we were still sinners . . . even while we were yet unborn! There is nothing — nothing — I can do to make God quit loving me. He can't *not* love me. His love is both unconditional and irrevocable. And it's not based in any way whatsoever on what I do. God loves because God is love.

2. My relationship with God is conditional.

While His love is unconditional, my relationship with God is two-way. Love can be unilateral. A relationship, however, is bilateral. For instance, I might insist that nothing my wife could ever do would change my love — I love her unconditionally and irrevocably, yet a true relationship is two-way. What if she were to walk out on me and run off with another man, totally rejecting me and everything I stood for? Would I still love her? Yes, I could love her, if my love were unconditional. But would we still have a relationship? That's another question.

A relationship is bilateral: "It takes two." Love can go one way, but a relationship is two-way. Relationships are ongoing dynamic sorts of things which take two (at least partially) willing persons. Someone might argue that this immoral wife still had some legal standing with her husband, but most of us would admit that a pattern of continual and repeatedly purposeful acts of rebellion would end the two-way-ness of the relationship. My love might live on . . . but my marriage relationship would be dead. Relationships are not unilateral.

3. But Christians have great security.

A two-way relationship does not mean that Christians have little security. On the contrary, the security of a believer is exceptionally high — almost absolute. The chances of a real believer walking away from

God in rebellion and losing his own soul are remote. Remote, yet possible. Even in the highest state of grace we will always have free will, allowing us to reject God and ultimately lose our own souls.

But the chances of a real Christian eventually losing his own soul are slim. Why? Because His seed remains within us (1 John 3:9). At conversion we experienced a sort of "spiritual gene splicing." God's nature was planted inside us. We received a tendency to be godly. Sure, it is possible for us to disobey Him. But spiritual rebellion — the hardened, set-chin spiritual defiance which breaks a relationship — is a very unlikely happening for a truly born-again Christian.

A continual pattern of purposeful, premeditated disobedience will indeed eventually harden into an attitude of rebellion and defiance — and that can break off our two-way relationship with God. But the likelihood of you doing this is minimal. Rather, you have a great security in Christ. High security. Immense security. Almost unconditional — but not quite.

4. Our daily relationship with God is the better focus.

The relationship we have with God is ongoing and dynamic, not just a legal covenant established long ago. The middle-of-the-road security focuses on a daily, developing walk with God, not just a once-for-all event that occurred years ago. Like a marriage, our daily relationship with God is quite as important as the initiating event. The marriage is quite as important as the wedding.

The practical middle-of-the-road approach is to focus on a daily, growing walk with God where the issue of security need never come up. Are you developing a loving, growing, bilateral marriage relationship? If so, the chances of such a relationship dissolving are remote. Are you developing a loving, growing, bilateral relationship with God? If so, the chances of such a relationship dissolving are also remote.

The security is not just in the initiating event, wedding or conversion. It is in a growing, loving relationship. And, the best news yet: God is even more forbearing than your spouse!

1. How secure do you think a Christian really is? If you were making a continuum, where would you place yourself on the line between the two extremes?

2. What are the dangers of the two extremes?

3. What Scriptures appear to support absolute security? What Scriptures appear to support the idea that a Christian could indeed rebel against God and leave God's family?

4. What are the practical differences in daily life between the two extremes? How would either extreme deal with failure, sin, broken relationships?

5. Think about the consequences of being wrong in both instances. What if those who believe in eternal security are wrong? What if those who do not believe in eternal security are wrong?

6. Where is the common ground on which Christians of both positions can meet and agree here (especially as it relates to dealing with Christians who fall into sin).

The Outback Steak-Church

After eating a delicious steak dinner with our best friends recently, I couldn't help but wonder what church planting would look like if done with the Outback Steak House method. Here's what I think you'd do.

1. You'd limit your programming.

Conventional wisdom in the restaurant business is to find a good location, operate as many hours as possible to spread the fixed costs, and keep the food costs as low as possible. The Outback Steak House breaks all three rules. When Chris Sullivan and Robert Basham started the chain, they wanted to have some life beyond steakhouse management for their two interests: boating and golf. Figuring their managers should get the same, they determined the Outbacks would only be open in the evenings for one shift a day. They thought offering everything all the time would water down the product. They decided to be open fewer hours and do the job better. What they discovered was both the waiting staff and their managers avoided burnout (average industry manager turnover = 35%; Outback turnover = 5.4%). The point: do less and do it better.

The Outback Steak-Church would benefit from this philosophy of doing less and doing it better — and thus avoid pastoral/staff burnout.

2. You'd limit the seating.

Most Americans, steak lovers and otherwise, prefer to dream big and build likewise. Hey, if you've got people lined up and waiting two hours for a steak dinner, what would you do? Tear down your building and put up a bigger building, right? Not at the Outback. The typical Outback is 6,000 square feet (with the kitchen taking more than half of that) and seats only 220. Only 220. Why? Because, according to Sullivan and Basham, that's the optimum seating to guarantee a quality steak. Great Steak is their goal — everything else serves the Great Steak goal. If one restaurant can no longer accommodate a growing crowd, they just plant more Outback steakhouses in new locations. Which is exactly what they've done to the tune of more than 200 new steakhouses in the last five years. They argue that an optimum facility is better than a gigantic one.

An Outback Steak-Church doesn't tear down the old building and put up a new sanctuary. It decides on an optimum size and then spins off new churches.

3. You'd recruit people with certain qualities, then train them for competence.

A friendly, decentralized "flat" company, the Outback is committed to a friendly, informal atmosphere. When they hire, they worry more about a candidate's friendliness than his or her previous experience. Instead of recruiting experienced cooks and waiters, the Outback hires 75 to 80 friendly people, then trains them to cook and serve. They believe it is easier to add competence to friendliness than the reverse.

The application for the Outback Steak-Church is obvious.

4. You'd treat your workers well.

Outback managers only work from 3:00 p.m. to midnight and make about $120,000 a year doing what they love. The Outback's waiters start later yet and earn about $125 a night. Both work only one shift straight through. Morale is high among the managers and staff.

An Outback Steak-Church values its workers, makes sure they know that their intangible, eternal rewards are far greater than a mere paper $120,000. Morale would be high, the staff would stay put, and the Sunday school teachers would love their work.

5. You'd serve first-rate Steak (preaching-teaching).

The Outback serves Steak with a capital S. You don't go there for desserts or vegetables. You go for Steak. Every Outback Steak grew up in a particular area of either Nebraska or Colorado known to produce the tastiest Steaks. Sure, conventional wisdom declares that people are eating less red meat, but the Outback folk know better. If you serve great

Steak, prepared well and seasoned delightfully, people will wait two hours to get a seat.

Conventional wisdom dictates that what people really want from the pulpit is entertainment. The Outback Steak-Church knows that if you preach and teach the Word of God according to the highest standards, people will fill the sanctuary.

It just might work.

1. The conventional wisdom is that people want fluff and little five-point tips for living sermons. Others say that there are still plenty of people who want the meat of the Word in preaching. What do you think?

2. Churches usually feel compelled "to do everything" instead of narrowing their focus and simply saying, "We don't offer that." Why do you think churches tend to be this way? Is it good? Bad?

3. If you could pick an "optimum size" for your own church, what would that be?

4. Why did you not pick a larger number?

5. What single thing could your church do to "treat our workers better"?

6. If you followed the Outback model for recruiting leaders in your church, what qualities would you seek?

THE END TIMES HOBBY

Having received my thousandth e-mail announcing the second coming as March 10th, 1997, it is time I wrote back. What is it about the Web that inspires people to come up with such complicated formulas as: William Jefferson Clinton combined with Hillary Rodham Clinton totals 666? As if that were not enough, they are then inspired by some spirit to send their inside information to umpteen million people: "Pssssst Read this! The latest tells me the Prince of Wales is indeed the Antichrist, meeting 27 of 42 possible signs."

As a veteran of times when evangelists unfolded intricately painted, canvas time-maps across the front of little churches and of more recent fads like *88 Reasons Christ Will Return in 1988*, I take a dim view of these date-setters. They clutter up my mailbox and waste the time I could use to write to real people about real problems.

So, I've decided to write a response which my mail system can send automatically to these dear hearts. Here it is.

Bless you for sending me mail about religious matters, but I won't be reading your letter. I don't read end-times or date-setting e-mails. Here's why:

1. I think you End-Timers have too much time on your hands.

Maybe I'm wrong about this, but I feel that you are wasting time that should be spent elsewhere. Instead of speculating about the date of the second coming, I wish you'd volunteer to teach a Junior Sunday school class, or work in a mission, or sign up for nursery duty. It's not that I have the right to tell you how to spend your time. I don't. I waste time too (such as writing a weekly essay or this reply to you). It's just that of all the people I know who dwell on this subject, most are dreamer speculators who do little of the actual work of the church. They'd rather figure out numerological puzzles than shovel snow or clean up the fellowship hall. So, I won't be reading your conjectures — I'll be preparing my Sunday school lesson, or doing something else more constructive.

2. Endtiming is not evangelistic.

You claim to enhance evangelism, I know. Your idea is that I should start telling people that Jesus will return March 10th, and they'll get scared enough to become Christians. Or, knowing the date is close, I will be motivated to act right. But it won't work. Not really. And even if some are saved, they'll likely wind up being like the shallow-soil conversions which fizzle later (especially by March 11th, if He does not return on the 10th). The whole idea is like telling the fellow who is cheating on his wife, "She's gonna walk through that door in three hours!" Would this change anything? HA! Most cheaters would figure out they had two hours and forty-five minutes to play around. The same applies to sinners. Knowing the date of the second coming does not change immediate behavior for the better. Frankly, if the unsaved won't listen now, they wouldn't listen even if someone rose from the dead to tell them.

3. Quit telling me you have inside information from God.

Hey, c'mon . . . I don't even believe the Pope when he says that. Stop it!

4. Why place so much value on dates?

This is a case of misplaced priorities. You are like the Magi — spiritual astrologers seeking answers from your sky of numbers. The attention should be on God and Christ and the gospel. You trivialize these more weighty matters by emphasizing dates and crazy 666 theories.

5. Your ignorance of history is showing.

You tell me things like: the last verse in the last chapter of the last book of the Bible is the exact same number as the birth year and birth date of your most recent nomination for Antichrist. Doesn't it bother you that the verse numbers were not even added until 1551? In fact, it probably *doesn't* bother you, for you have such a broad view of inspiration that you claim it for yourself. Yours is a too-low view of the Scriptures and a too-high view of man.

6. I resist End-Timers' humanist tendencies.

Face it, the whole thing is about *figuring out* God's plans. To figure out things best left in God's realm places too much emphasis on man and man's intellect. Can you figure out for yourself what Christ claimed only the Father knew? What if you did? What would this accomplish, other than to show your own human cleverness? Are you greater than Christ? Do you know the things He himself assigned only to the Father? Do you want us to worship you? Are you greater than He? Sorry, even if you are right, I'll stick with Jesus.

7. So what?

What if you are indeed right about the second coming happening this March 10th (or June 27th, or December 21st)? So what? What good does it do to know this? Would it change anything? Would it cause Christians to quit school, stop working, begin carrying placards on the streets, go visit all their relatives and witness to them? Would it? If so, then why don't we do these things now? Isn't that the gist of all of Jesus' teaching on these matters? He taught us to keep our lamps trimmed, to keep a supply of oil every day. Feed the hungry, clothe the naked, visit those who are sick and in prison — and to do these things on a daily basis, as if *every* day was The Day of the Lord. We are not to act like students prompted to cram just before the final exam.

Sorry. I'll pass on your end-times letter. Rather, I want to live every single day as if it is the last. This is the way Jesus taught, in my opinion. Your opinion may differ and that is fine. But I don't have to read your unsolicited mail either. Knowing the real date would not improve things for me, other than give me the impression that I have plenty of time before March 10th (to prepare my lamps and care for the poor before the sheep and goats are sorted out). No, I'd rather live as if tomorrow were the day, not as if I have several months to spare. So I'll pass on reading about dates and signs and speculative myths or numerology. Many of us in the Kingdom of God feel that we have more important things to do than play spiritual Stratego.

God bless you, just the same.

1. What is it that causes such fascination with date-setting and figuring out who the Beast or Antichrist is?

2. What are the dangers of being hardened against end-times warnings?

3. What Scriptures would you quote to prove that no man can know the time of the second coming?

4. What actual difference should such studies make in the daily life of the Christian?

5. What are the signs of a spiritually unhealthy obsession about end times?

6. What are legitimate ways to study end times matters, and how should you tell others about such things?

IS IT TIME TO GIVE UP ON CAMPMEETINGS?

I t's hard to "hold your own" as a campmeeting anymore. From what I have observed, campmeetings are either flourishing or they are dying out. In some denominations they have already disappeared completely. In other denominations or districts they are holding on by the skin of their teeth. In a few they are flourishing and even growing. But even where they are growing, they face increasing opposition and lack of support. Some churches become "client churches" while other churches completely ignore the camp, and even try to close it down.

Why are camps having trouble in some districts? I don't have the answers. But for 23 years in a row, I have spoken at several camps per summer, so I have a few ideas. Some of the factors influencing decline in the campmeeting in my opinion are:

1. Upward economic drift.

Our people are better off than they used to be, and not just in the sense that we are all better off. Holiness churches have drifted up the economic ladder a few rungs. There are exceptions, of course, but generally the higher up on this ladder your people get, the less excited they'll be about campmeeting.

2. Third rate planning.

The campmeetings which are declining have no first-rate planners (who are usually busy running their own local churches), and often even few second-tier planners/leaders. In the declining campmeetings, the program is run by third-rate planners who couldn't get any other job. The first-line leaders just do cameos for a few days or for the evening meetings only.

3. Failure to keep up.

In their heyday in the nineteenth century, camps had outdoor toilets — but people of that time period had outdoor toilets at home too. In homes today, however, few people share their bathrooms with strangers or walk 100 yards to take a shower. In some areas where the camping/hunting culture prevails, this is no problem. But where such a culture does not exist, the campgrounds that haven't kept up are often declining.

4. No "special" purpose.

The original purpose of the brush arbors was frontier evangelism. Then the holiness movement adopted the campmeeting as its "special" means of propagating a second work of grace. But few campmeetings do much serious evangelism anymore. And only a few still insist that every message — morning, afternoon and evening — be about holiness. Fellowship and unity-building/reunion are the only clear purposes for many campmeetings today, but even these purposes are not clearly articulated or promoted. Like many Sunday evening services, campmeetings are often meetings without a clear purpose.

5. They are too long.

Fewer and fewer people are willing to go away for an entire week or ten days for a campmeeting — certainly not for two weeks! The best speakers in the nation won't come for eight days, or even five days. So most campmeetings no longer get the best speakers. They are stuck with those willing to come for ten days or a week. Granted, some camps are now "splitting the camp" between speakers — getting one speaker for the first half of camp and a second one for the last four days. But even these camps can't get the number one speakers in the nation (who are all off speaking for one hour at Promise Keepers).

6. Larger churches.

There was a time when camps supplied the best speakers and music any of the people had heard all year long. This is no longer true. We now have a host of larger and mid-size churches that have better music, speakers and programming than the district camps. Campmeetings no longer offer the annual benchmark of excellence in many districts.

7. Diminishing emphasis on "crisis theology."

Campmeetings have always been about going to the altar, making a decision. Campmeetings were first about "getting saved" and later about "getting sanctified" or some combination of both crisis experiences. As more and more holiness people and pastors adopted a more gradual approach to both sanctification and conversion, the need for the high pressure, hard-sell altar call of the campmeeting diminished.

8. Disappearance of the professional evangelist.

Who speaks at camps? Professional evangelists? No, we now use pastors, district superintendents, college people, and headquarters people. These are all fine folk, but they are surely not the "hired gun" type of professional evangelists we once used at campmeetings. In fact most all of today's best "professional" speakers are one-shot/one-hour speakers. Thus events like Gaither's Praise Gathering or Promise Keepers scoop them up — not for an eight-day series, but five or six of them, back to back over two or three days, one hour each. Many "top-notch" speakers are glad to come for an hour. (What a life!) The old professional evangelist stirred up loyalty to campmeetings. Many of today's campmeeting speakers (though most will not admit it) do not even believe very much in campmeeting themselves.

9. Lack of spiritual hunger.

Do you know a lot of people so spiritually hungry that they will use their vacation from work to stay at a campmeeting to hear preaching and teaching three times a day for two weeks straight? My granddad did. And he did it before he was saved! I don't see that much hunger around today. I see some short bursts of temporary hunger, maybe for some "fast-food spirituality." But not much hunger for a two-week banquet. Campmeetings fight this lack of interest now more than ever. A good swimming pool might help, but . . . preaching?

10. Government regulations.

It is getting harder to keep a campmeeting grounds open for just a few weeks a year. It is still possible, but getting more difficult. And renting someone else's grounds loses that "sacred space" magnetism.

11. Middle-age spread.

My own denomination, like others, does not have a consistent product across the church, as a whole — or even in a district. We are not like

McDonald's, where a quarter pounder tastes like a quarter pounder in every outlet. We are old enough to have developed quite a variety of opinions — many deeply held — on worship styles, music, and even preaching. This "middle-age spread" in styles is making it increasingly difficult for a district campmeeting to present music, worship and preaching which fills the bill for all churches. Some are likely to consider what you do quaint and old-fashioned, while others believe you are "pushing the envelope" too far. So some camps find the safest common ground is to select the music and worship style of thirty years ago. Then the more progressive churches can bring their kids to show them how it used to be, like visiting a spiritual flea market.

12. Subsidies.

When the people are no longer willing to pay for camp, the denominational district or conference will have to dip into its regular funds to subsidize camp. When and if this happens, eventually some will come to treat campmeeting as a welfare mother living off subsidies. They will look for any reason to swoop down on the camp and close it. The camps which thrive best are those the people gladly support.

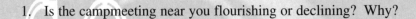

1. Is the campmeeting near you flourishing or declining? Why?

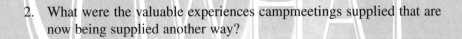

2. What were the valuable experiences campmeetings supplied that are now being supplied another way?

3. If campmeetings as we have known them are dying out, what has replaced them?

4. What other factors have contributed to the decline or success of campmeetings as you know them?

5. If you could make the decision for your denomination on campmeetings, what would you do?

IT'S
FRIIIIIIIIDAY!

Like many Protestants, Good Friday has never been a big deal to me. When I was a kid, all my Catholic friends and some Lutheran ones made a big affair out of it. My church didn't. Easter Sunday was our special day (maybe because we already attended church on Sunday, so it was easier). Good Friday required something extra. But I was told this downplaying of Good Friday was theological too. I was taught that the Resurrection was the validating event for Good Friday: "If Christ be not raised, your faith is vain" (1 Cor. 15:17 KJV). It was as if "the more you believe in Easter, the less you'll believe in Good Friday." They said, "The Catholics never get Jesus off the cross; we believe in a resurrected Christ." Or, "We're an Easter church, not a Good Friday church." (They, of course, were wrong about that because if my denomination had to pick a day, we'd have been a "Pentecost" church, if anything.)

But I still wonder why many Protestants make so little of Good Friday. We vote with Tony . . . it's Friiiiiiiiiiiday! And everything is dark and looks like all will be lost. Let's get it over with!

However, I wonder if there's another factor. Easter is easier to "sell" to people so desperate for uplifting thoughts. Easter is bright, sunny, exciting and full of hope. It is about joy, excitement, discovery and new life. That sells today. Friday is about pain, agony, blood and death. No wonder many of us don't make a big deal about Good Friday.

However, the focus of Christian theology is not just on an unoccupied Sunday morning tomb, but also on an occupied Friday cross. I feel the need for more "Good Friday" in my life, even though it is not a pick-me-up day. I've paid a price for downplaying Good Friday.

1. Downplaying Good Friday allows me to downplay SIN.

That's what the cross is about. On Friday I am reminded that I am a sinner, that I've broken God's law. I am guilty . . . stained . . . convicted. I've been "bad." Frankly, I'd rather be told how great I am, how wonderful humanity is, what great potential I have. These things encourage me, build me up. I feel better hearing more about self-esteem and less about self-sacrifice. It's hard to do that on Friiiiiiiiiiday.

2. Downplaying Good Friday allows me to downplay JUDGMENT.

Because of my sin I am guilty of death . . . "the wages of sin is death" (Rom. 6:23). On Friday I see the wrath of God — not a twisted vindictiveness, or unloving rage, but a certain justice for sin. In God there is nothing irreconcilable between wrath and love. Such problems occur only in my limited thinking. God is just and therefore will punish sin. He is not a doting, grandfatherly Mister-Rogers-in-the-sky who overlooks sin and reassures us that we are fine just the way we are. He is loving, caring and gentle, yet at the same time angry, wrathful, jealous, and a sure punisher of sin. Friday reminds me of my just desserts: hell. I don't like to talk about hell, especially in relation to me. Mentioning hell from the pulpit seems impolite, indelicate, unrefined. I much prefer a God something like . . . well, uh . . . maybe like Phil Donahue — understanding, helpful, kind, and very broad-minded, especially when it comes to me personally. People don't like to think about hell. When they think of dying, they prefer to think of moving serenely through a dark tunnel at the end of which they meet a bright, accepting, warm light. They see eternity as sort of like going to Florida. I'd rather hear about nicer things than judgment. It's hard to do that on Friiiiiiiiiiday.

3. Downplaying Good Friday allows me to downplay the BLOOD.

If I am a sinner deserving judgment, even hell, how shall I escape? Through the blood of Christ. On Good Friday I am reminded that we are "saved by the blood of the Lamb." It seems so crude to the modern mind — saved by "blood." We wonder, how will the animal-rights activists respond? The Cross is an offense to good taste. Blood — from His head, His hands, His feet and His side. Blood spilled for me. Not a pretty picture. But it is a picture of the gospel as Saint Paul saw it — and as most others have for 2000 years. Good Friday is a "bloody sort of day." Taking a day to focus on a bloody, torn corpse hanging on a cross on some distant hill in the past is not pleasant work. Not as fun as dressing up and taking a pretty lily home from church. But the blood is what you get on Friiiiiiiiiiday.

But this Friday, I'll halt my normal activities and think about these things just the same. I think it will be good for me — especially about the blood of Christ.

I'll be happy that my sins are *"covered by the blood."*
I'll be rejoicing that, like the children of Israel, I will escape for:
"When I see the blood, I will pass over you."
I'll thank God this Friday that:
"There is a fountain filled with blood
Drawn from Immanuel's veins;
And sinners, plunged beneath that flood,
Lose all their guilty stains."

After all, the real question about my own sin is:
"What can wash away my sin?
Nothing but the blood of Jesus;
What can make me whole again?
Nothing but the blood of Jesus."

And I might even turn dark, gloomy Good Friday into a time of praise:
"When I saw the cleansing fountain, Open wide for all my sin,
I obeyed the Spirit's wooing, When He said, Wilt thou be clean?
I will praise Him! I will praise him!
Praise the Lamb for sinners slain;
Give Him glory, all ye people,
For His blood can wash away each stain."

I'll be thinking mostly of the old songs I learned as a kid (when a person's theology is molded without your knowing it). Like,

"Down at the cross where my Savior died.
Down where for cleansing from sin I cried,
There to my heart was the blood applied;
Glory to His name!"

So on next Good Friday I'll be thinking about sin, and judgment, and especially about the blood of Christ. It is a day more suited for the Lord's Supper, than yard work or in-line skating. To me, I am coming to believe that observing Easter without Good Friday teaches a half-truth.

Maybe if I observe Good Friday right, Easter will mean more than bunnies, Easter baskets and a new set of clothes.

1. Which day has been downplayed more in your own tradition — Good Friday or Easter Sunday?

2. What are the just-as-serious losses in downplaying Easter Sunday?

3. What ideas have you heard of for observing Good Friday?

4. What role might our culture play in the observance of these two days (Friday being a normal workday, while Sunday is a day off for most people)?

5. List all the theological elements relating to what happened on Good Friday and what happened on Easter Sunday.

6. Easter Sunday is also a secular holiday . . . why doesn't Good Friday have a secular equivalent? What are the implications of this?

DO YOU EVER GET DISCOURAGED ABOUT THE CHURCH?

Ever look around the church and get discouraged? I do. The Enemy seems to be making gains on all fronts. However, consider how you'd feel if you were on the other side — the Enemy's side. Put yourself in the shoes of one committed to destroying Christian faith. You might be thinking something like this:

These Christians are a stubborn lot, almost impossible to get rid of. For 20 centuries we've tried to stomp them out yet, in spite of our efforts, they've spread their religion to every corner of the world. It's an awfully hard religion to destroy — you cut off a head, and twenty grow back.

You persecute them, and they go underground and develop a purer strain of their religion. You kill them and they build on their martyrs' blood. Get them to water down their faith, and a little group somewhere will rediscover the real faith and they'll start over again. They have an infuriating way of regenerating themselves!

And these Christians know how to turn a negative into a positive. They turn our best laid plans upside down. Get a couple of their famous religious figures to commit adultery or visit a prostitute, and they'll simply produce a thousand seminars and books on sexual fidelity. The net effect will be greater morality among many of them, not lesser. It's discouraging!

Denominations are, of course, good targets. However, as quickly as one cools off, they'll start a new one. These Christians produce new denominations faster than roaches reproduce baby roaches. Same with local churches. No sooner do we get a local church to die spiritually than there'll be two brand-new ones cropping up in some school auditorium across town. It's hopeless, I tell you!

A few times in history we've pretty well got the whole church to go lukewarm. Then along comes a John Wesley or a John Knox, and a whole nation turns back to God. Even when all of organized religion is waning, they go out and launch a new strain of pure Christianity in some religious order or para-church organization.

Make 'em poor, and they praise God. Make them rich, and someone like St. Francis will come along and teach them to live the opposite way. Get them totally absorbed with their fancy buildings and elegant worship, and some Quaker-like group will sprout up and reintroduce a religion of simplicity and plainness. Close all their buildings and lock their doors, and they'll shrug their shoulders and move into homes, declaring it to be an improvement. Close a nation to missionaries, and they'll just sneak in as tentmakers, and infect people one at a time. Kick out all the missionaries and suppress Christianity like we did in China, and what do we get? Twenty-five years later there are several hundred thousand committed Christians who simply practiced their faith underground. They're hard to get rid of, I tell you.

Introduce division and strife among the churches and they'll invent something like Promise Keepers or these new Citywide Worship Events and restore a sense of unity. Divide them and they multiply; create strife and they make peace. And they've got money — lots of money! They give billions every week! That's B as in Billions, and W as in every Week. Christianity is the largest single economic enterprise in the world, dwarfing pip-squeak outfits like General Motors. Millions of them give ten percent of their income every week. It adds up! Just think what would happen if non-believers were that committed.

And they support a zillion different enterprises: colleges and universities to train millions of their youth; radio programs up and down the dial — even entire radio stations now — and they sponsor TV programs, bookstores, publishing houses, seminars, training programs. They even have their own full line of Christian music. I tell you, it's discouraging for us non-believers at times. As soon as our side gets hold of a new medium, Christians come running alongside and swamp us with their Christian message. Look what they did with books, radio and TV. My goodness, who knows what they'll do on the Internet!

We do have one advantage. Christians are easy to get off track. But the discouraging thing is, once we've got them sidetracked, a whole new wave comes along and gets the church back on track — it's as if there is an invisible spirit of some sort correcting and guiding them. It's discouraging, I tell you!

How do we crush these Christians out of existence? It's not easy, I tell you. Rome couldn't do it. The Dark Ages didn't do it. State religion didn't do it. Darwin couldn't either. Rationalism couldn't. Neither could liberalism, communism, socialism, democracy, nor modernity. You can't tax them into oblivion, or legislate them out of existence. And if you ignore them, they won't go away. I tell you, they're hard to beat!

Divide them and they'll unify. Beat them down and they pop back up. Create strife and they make peace. Criticize them and they listen with a smile. Hate them and they love you back. Take their coats and they'll give you their cloaks too. Persecute them and they'll multiply; arrest them and they witness to you; beat them and they sing; kill them and they simply go to heaven. I tell you, you can't beat them! Talk about discouragement!

Since you can't beat them . . . why not join them?

1. Do Christians sometimes think the church is far worse off than it really is? Why?

2. What would you add to this list of encouraging factors for all Christians to rejoice about?

3. What factors have gotten church folk down recently? Is there an encouraging "flip side" to these factors?

4. What dangerous sidetracks have appeared in the last ten years or so? Is there such a sidetrack currently misleading Christians?

5. Can you recall an incident from history or your own life where God turned things upside down, making a positive out of a negative?

6. What encourages you most as you look at Christ's church around the world today?

WHY IN THE WORLD WOULD A SUPER-CHURCH PASTOR LEAVE?

W hen Chuck Swindoll, John Maxwell and Dale Galloway left their local churches as pastors, many of us began asking, "Why would a pastor leave a super church where he seems to have everything you could hope for?" With a bit of thought and some discussion several reasons began to emerge. Such as:

1. Pastoring a super church is exhausting work.

Pastoring a big church might mean a big salary, big fame and a big staff, but it also means big criticism, big problems and big headaches. The assumption that they've "got it made" is inaccurate — a myth the rest of us make up about them, like peasants dreaming how good it is to be king. It is more common than you'd think for super-church pastors to privately confess a frequent yearning for the days "when they pastored that church of 125 they used to have." These guys have left hard work. Very hard work.

2. They have reached a pivotal age.

Maybe they're tired. Two of them said as much in their resignations. Guys in their 50s and 60s can't run at the same pace they did at age 40. All three of these guys were burning the candle at both ends. Maybe they're getting worried about the wax.

3. Theirs is a John Wesley mentality.

There are simply some men whose ministry can't be limited to any one place — the "world is their parish," so they increasingly act like it.

4. Finances.

Certainly this can't be a primary factor — any more than you taking your present ministry for money. But money sometimes is an ancillary consideration. If a pastor makes a bundle of money and buys a fancy house, he gets severely criticized (as Swindoll did). But if you operate a business — even a religious one — and make a bundle, you are simply thought to be smart. Maybe one or more of these guys wants to become financially independent before he retires. It's a possibility.

5. The grind.

Pastoring slowly grinds one down. Preparing new messages every week. Making hard decisions. Raising money. Making plans. Pacifying people. Visiting hospitals (well, maybe not hospital visitation in these cases). And dealing with the same old people, at the same old building, in the same old town. We forget that the weekly grind is still there for the "big guys." In a para-church ministry you can fly in, drop the record on a perfectly honed, candy stick sermon, be treated like a king, then fly out and not have to deal with the messy stuff of local pastoring. I know this . . . I do it. Perhaps the grind just finally got to them.

6. A shift in the definition of success?

Has there been a subtle shift in the definition of success over the last few years? Is serving as a super-church pastor no longer the "top of the heap" in our pyramidal minds? Has pastoring a super church lost some luster? If it has, some super-church pastors may wonder, "Why kill myself like this if it isn't really impressing anybody that much anymore?"

7. But even if we still measure "success" by money and staff . . .

The largest budgets and staffs are not in local churches. If we use these secular definitions for success, then the real top bananas are the men who preside over the para-church and quasi-church ministries. Consider Pat Robertson, who rules a ministry with an income of three million dollars a week. A week! Or how about James Dobson? What local church pastor has a two-million-a-week income, a staff of 1300, and spends $163,000 to send out his midweek mailing?! So, the really big fish in today's pond aren't super-church pastors, but Promise Keeper speakers who have their own organizations. Even if the definition of "success" is still secular, all three of these men will be more "successful" outside the local church.

8. Vision ceiling.

Super-church pastors are usually men (no women yet) of great vision. They are also men of great impatience. They want things to happen — now! Sometimes pastors move on simply because they are not seeing things move as fast as they'd like. We know this is true of "regular" pastors. But it is also true of super-church pastors. It is always easier to cast a vision than to complete it. Sometimes (all the time?) the people don't move as fast as the vision expands. Downsizing a vision is painful work.

9. Maybe God told them to change.

Without trying to figure out the human reasons, we all have to accept the fact that God sometimes calls ministers to do something different. He has you, right? Maybe God called all three of these guys to get out of the local church. At least we need to give them the benefit of the doubt. I've noticed that most ministers explain their *own* reasons for leaving by talking about God's leading, but suggest that other ministers leave because of human factors like #1-8 above. God's direct call is a possibility you've got to allow for others too. Maybe God calls men to move on, both because He has other work for these men, and because He wants to make room for the other men (and women) He is raising up.

10. Condensed ministry.

Maybe the half-life of a super-church pastor is shorter than that of "regular pastors." Maybe they're like baseball players — they give their decade or two, then do something else for the rest of their lives. If so, I'd say all three of these guys "played good ball" while they were in the game. I hate to see them go. However, I'm glad I got to see them play.

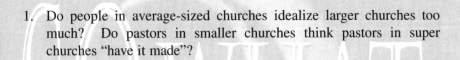

1. Do people in average-sized churches idealize larger churches too much? Do pastors in smaller churches think pastors in super churches "have it made"?

2. How do you feel about the whole idea of "super churches" or famous pastors?

3. Which of these factors might affect an ordinary, non-famous pastor's decision to leave a church?

4. On the average, when a pastor makes a decision to leave a church, what percentage do you think is God's leading and what percentage can be attributed to other factors . . . on the average, that is.

5. How do you think ministers' "career" decisions differ from those of laity?

My Pet Peeve: Flags in Church

27

Everybody ought to have a personal religious pet peeve. You know, something that really bugs you, or gets under your skin. Do you have something that rubs you the wrong way at church? I do. Some people's pet peeve concerns the announcements or the way the Scripture is read (or not read). Others get worked up when told to raise their hands or clap. Still others specialize in screening the message to pounce on any grammatical errors. Others get irritated about the sound system or lighting level. Music, of course, offers the best opportunity for pet peeves of all kinds. Having a pet peeve is nice. It gives you something to think about during lulls in the service.

My pet peeve is flags; that is, flags displayed in churches. Most American churches, like the German churches of the 1930s, flaunt their flags right up front with other symbols like the communion table, Bible, and cross, so I get bugged just about every time I go to church. I grumble to myself, wondering why American churches insist on displaying a nationalistic symbol in their churches? What does it mean? That we practice some sort of civil religion? That America is somehow a Christian nation or is especially favored by God? Does it mean we believe, "my country right or wrong"? Or, are we telling ourselves that we're "American Christians" not "world Christians"? If a flag is a symbol, then what does it symbolize? I think about these kinds of things

133

during the 16th repetition of a chorus or during the reading of the announcements.

What are flags? People salute them, pledge allegiance to them, and sometimes follow them to their deaths. A flag is a powerful symbol — a symbol of loyalty and allegiance. And like all powerful symbols, there is an explicit code for display. For instance, on a two-flag pole the top flag represents the "higher" loyalty or greater authority. In a meeting hall or church, the flag on the right represents the "higher" allegiance. Thus, if a church displays flags on the platform, the flag to the right of the pulpit is the greater authority. If the flags are on the floor, the one to the right of the audience represents the highest loyalty.

So what's my peeve here? It is this: in 25 years of traveling and speaking, almost half of the churches I've visited display the American flag so that it has higher authority over the Christian flag. What???? I mumble under my breath, "What in the world does this mean?" Is such a church really saying that their loyalty to the country is greater than loyalty to God? Yikes! Sometimes I've almost forgotten what I was supposed to speak about. Of course it could be simple ignorance — maybe they don't know the code. But if that is so, then why display flags at all?

Then there are those clever churches that display the Christian flag to the right of the speaker, then put the American flag on the floor to the right of the audience — presto, both in places of precedence. It's a clever compromise, but what does this mean? That the preacher puts the Kingdom first, and the people put the nation first? That's a screwy notion and not much better.

Even when a church puts the Christian flag in the place of primacy, I get to thinking about why they display the nationalistic symbol at all. I keep wondering if they'd display an eagle on the communion table or, if they were Germans in 1939, they'd put swastikas on the wall beside the cross. To me, any nationalistic symbol seems out of place in the church of God.

OK, I know I'm overdoing this. After all, that's what a pet peeve is all about, making mountains out of molehills. And I know that medieval churches often mixed Bible images, national flags and images of local patrons in their stained glass windows. (They also burned people up who disagreed with their doctrine.) I just don't see what flags add to worship. Does it help us focus on God better? Not me. I find myself focusing on the flag.

Now this whole hang-up is generally only a low-grade irritant. The only time it gets serious is when I visit some Bill Hybels wannabe's church, where they've stripped away all the Christian symbols from the 50-year-old church, removed the cross from the front wall, shoved the communion table into a back room, and obliterated all other Christian symbols — yet keep the American flag. Now, what in the world does this mean?

I know, many of you will chide me for nursing such a minor peeve (except, of course, you Quakers or Mennonites who are smiling broadly at my enlightenment). I've discovered that other people's pet peeves are almost always minor things; only my own seem really important. Maybe that's true for you too?

Anyway, I know I should be thinking about loftier things than flags in church. But it *is* my pet religious peeve. I've kept it secret for several decades and am just now letting it out. You're really not supposed to tell people your pet peeve. Why? Because then it becomes a complaint. I don't want to be a complainer. To me, peeves should be personal things, something you can grumble to yourself about, not share with others — that's the fun of it.

So now that I've gone public with my flag pet peeve, I'll be needing a new one that I can keep private. Maybe you can help me — what's your pet peeve?

1. Why do you think the writer feels so strongly about the issue of nationalistic flags?

2. Are there countries where you think it would be inappropriate to display the national flag?

3. What would your own country have to do to make flag-display inappropriate?

4. Now, to the larger issue, one definition of a pet peeve is "an opinion you hold strongly about something most other people dismiss as trivial." What would your definition be?

5. What are some of the religious pet peeves you know about, or have yourself?

6. How can a person keep a pet peeve from ruining his attitude?

7. What do you think of the writer's idea that once you begin sharing your pet peeve it becomes a complaint and should be abandoned?

EVANGELISM'S COMEBACK

I admit I'm not the "evangelism type." In fact, I've always been a little suspicious of people who, for the sake of evangelism, "just stay near the door." I've always figured they stayed near the door because they really liked the outside better and wanted an excuse to live on the fringe of Christian commitment. But even a guy like me, who is more at home with the second half of the Great Commission than the first half, can notice the disappearance of evangelism from the evangelical church.

Billy Graham's massive Los Angeles evangelistic crusade is ancient history to most of my readers, but what followed a few decades later was the flourishing of personal evangelism. Some might remember the 1972 Campus Crusade's "Expo" in Dallas, or at least the fallout, as evangelical parrots learned to say, "Have you ever heard the four spiritual laws?" and promised, "God has a wonderful plan for your life." Denominations followed up with KEY '73, an interdenominational, cooperative evangelistic effort.

And I bet many of us still have somewhere in our library that nicely padded green book, *Evangelism Explosion* by D. James Kennedy. (Yes, young readers, back then Kennedy was better known for personal evangelism than politics and pipe organs.) If you can't recall these evangelism efforts, maybe you'll remember the "Here's Life" campaign, or after that, John Maxwell's GRADE program, which deployed laity going out door-to-door, to be "soul winners."

I don't know why, but most personal evangelism movements seem to eventually lose steam. Though never intended to be mass evangelism, Bill Hybels' "seeker movement" had that exact effect in many copycat churches. The emphasis switched from personal evangelism to attraction evangelism. Many of us tried to put on a service that would attract and hold "seekers," thus moving evangelism back to the platform and closer to Billy Graham's mass evangelism approach. We found that (if we could survive all the guff from traditionalists) we could put on a service that unbelievers would attend — even attend regularly.

But evangelism has a tendency to "morph." Over the last decade or so it morphed into . . . "church growth." Gradually our emphasis switched from winning souls to "growing the church."

The trouble is, some churches discovered it was a whale of a lot easier to get people to come to church than to get them saved — truly transformed. They were willing to settle for attendance and participation. Evangelicals hardly noticed that much of our "church growth" was merely crop rotation — we recruited easily bored Boomers from their less "exciting" churches into our own "more motivating" environments. With all of our preoccupation with "church growth," the lost world has hardly been touched by the gospel.

A core problem, of course, is theological. Something like despair has leaked into many churches. There is increasing doubt that God really can change lives. There is doubt about the value of an "instantaneous conversion" in bringing real deliverance. Instead, we increasingly rely more on recovery models. Redemption has been traded for recovery. Can God deliver people from habits? In a moment? Can He repair a marriage in a moment? Can God deliver a homosexual? Free us from lust? Maybe, but we doubt it. Our faith is weak. America's evangelical church is a modern day Nazareth.

But a sweeping change is coming. Maybe even a shake-out. The doctrine of transforming grace is a watershed — one worth thinking about, debating, restoring. I think we are on the verge of a great rediscovery of evangelism, because what we call evangelism today, isn't.

I bet we're going to see a renewed emphasis on conversion . . . not only as a change in legal status before God, but also as a transformational change in the individual's life . . . bringing a new and a changed life to the repentant.

And I'm betting we'll see a new emphasis on instantaneous conversion and deliverance. Since there's not much of that around now, it might even be considered a new idea. And it will probably be opposed by all of us who already know that God can't change people in less than twelve steps. But it's hard to put God in a box. Theology can't do it. Certainly psychology can't.

Also, I bet we'll see a renaissance of interest in conversion itself — in defining what really happens when a person is converted, how grace changes us, and how to know you really are converted. Who knows, some of our own members may get saved. Our soteriology is up for renewal.

All this brings me to a final point. I expect a new emphasis on evangelism to rush through the church in a couple of years — real evangelism, where sinners experience God's transforming grace . . . where God changes people . . . where old things pass away: old habits, old attitudes, old sins. And out of that we'll see a fresh wave of evangelistic fervor for a lost world.

But all this will have to start in the church. It probably won't be door-to-door, but pew-to-pew. Face it, most Christians need to become Christians. And it is so much more difficult to get Christians to become Christians than to get non-Christians to become Christians.

Will we see a return to transformational conversion?

1. Have you seen any evidence of the church's swing toward a more process-oriented view of conversion?

2. How would you define "evangelical"? Is it related to conversion? Conservative political views? What?

3. Why do more people seem to "get saved" gradually today than in the past? What is the cause of this change?

4. How does "gradual conversion" change how a person approaches evangelism?

5. The writer predicts a potential return to an emphasis on crisis conversion. Do you agree or disagree with this prediction? Why?

6. Can you cite the incidence of either gradual or instant conversion from the Bible?

WHAT TO DO WHEN A LEADER HAS AN AFFAIR

I mmorality within the church is not a new phenomenon, but in recent years Evangelicals have reeled as the affairs of prominent Christians have been graphically and publicly detailed. There may have been less smoke in the national media about the recent escapades of Christian musicians Michael English and Sandy Patti than the firestorm that surrounded the two "Jimmys" a few years earlier. That may mean simply that the national media is getting accustomed to such behavior within the Christian population, which in itself should be chilling news to Evangelicals. But we don't have to mention the names of a dozen or more other musicians and preachers to argue that there is a rash of this sort of thing going around.

Every pastor and church needs a principled plan for dealing with extramarital affairs. If you have not had a member or leader involved yet, it is only a matter of time. Sooner or later in your church you'll have to deal with someone in leadership who falls into sin and has an extramarital affair.

For instance, what would you do if a board member's daughter, who plays the piano in the services, simply moved in with her boyfriend? "But I love him," she says, and her parents insist that she continue playing because quitting would "discourage her and she might drop out of church." Would you let her continue? Or, say you pastored in a small village where your lay leader has been sneaking off to see a woman 20 years younger than he. Just about everyone in town knows it before you find out. You go to the board to remove him from leadership but they outvote you saying, "We need to forgive him." After the vote, he continues the affair, but at a reduced frequency. What would you do next? Or what if your music leader is caught in a homosexual affair but says he has been forgiven for it and wants to continue leading the choir. Would you let him continue?

If these stories sound real, it is because they are. If you don't have firm principles on this subject already established, you'll likely get blown about by the winds which surface at the time. While some of your people will argue for quick execution, you will be surprised at how many others will offer arguments for allowing the person to remain in leadership:

- God has forgiven them; why shouldn't we?
- They have stopped sinning; why hold a grudge against them now?
- The Bible says "judge not"; we should be accepting and loving, not judgmental.
- The individual should be our first concern, not a set of rules.
- What about Peter; he denied Christ, yet preached at Pentecost.
- Some gossip, others have affairs, both are equally sinful in God's sight.
- But she can sing (teach, give, etc.) so well; we need her.
- If we don't keep them, they'll just switch to XYZ church and be fully accepted.
- King David sinned just as bad, yet he stayed in power as king.
- The church is a place of redemption, not punishment.
- We should be like a city of refuge here, a safe haven for sinners.

These and other arguments will surely emerge the first time you confront an affair among the leadership of your church. If you do not have a set of principles, these winds will blow you one way and then another. What principles do you already have in place? Some denominations have clear principles and procedures. Are you committed to these? Will your district superintendent back you up?

I don't want to preempt the list of principles you might be making, but here is the list I use.

1. After an affair, a person must leave leadership. (No exceptions. I'll leave the church over this point.)

2. Adultery and gossip are not equal. (Breaking the marriage covenant is an exceptionally serious sin.)

3. The reputation of the church is a consideration, too. (We must be concerned with helping the individual, but not at the loss of the church's reputation [1 Cor. 5].)

4. Forgiveness does not mean allowing the fallen person to remain in leadership. (I might forgive a baby-sitter who sexually abused my daughter, but that does not mean I'll hire that person again.)

5. Restoring a fallen person as a Christian precedes restoring them as a leader. (The term "restoration" applies in both cases, but one comes first.)

6. Full restoration is possible. (After gaining forgiveness from God and others, dropping out of leadership for one or more years, and working through a restoration process, full restoration can occur — even restoration to leadership. In fact, I believe even a fallen ordained minister can be fully restored to active ministry. Sure, some of the people may never fully accept that person's ministry. [In fact, the probation period is mostly about facilitating a fallen leader's restoration in the mind of the church people, not God.] I personally think God's grace is great enough to enable a person to have a second chance — even at leadership. How? Not by ignoring or dismissing the sin. But by having that person drop out of leadership and deal with his sin.)

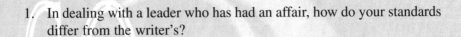

1. In dealing with a leader who has had an affair, how do your standards differ from the writer's?

2. What Scriptures would you turn to for guidance in deciding what to do in this matter?

3. How might your position differ if the offending person were your daughter or son?

4. This writer believes that after an affair a person can be restored to leadership, even the ministry. Many people disagree with this position. What do you think, and what Scripture supports your position?

5. If a person in your church has been caught committing adultery, then repented, placed himself/herself under discipline and accountability, and participated in a restoration process, do you think this person can eventually hold another leadership position? After a minimum of how long? For what offenses would you never restore a person to leadership?

ACOUSTIC WORSHIP

M any of us were raised on what we believed to be poorly planned, second-rate worship services. When we took over we determined to improve them, and we did. We decided that since people would no longer accept second-rate worship services, we would do everything first class. Along with the rest of our culture, we too went off "In Search of Excellence."

So, we installed first-rate sound boards, excellent lighting, bought a half-dozen mikes, and deployed a quality praise team to use them. We sidelined "sister Agnes," our local accompanist, in favor of perfectly crafted orchestral sound tracks for our soloists. They now sounded almost as good as the best singers in the country — so long as we played the sound track loud enough.

We avoided like AIDS the #1 enemy of production worship — DEAD AIR! Things whipped along nicely with our minute-by-minute schedule, with nary a moment of silence. We banished anything second rate and the resulting quality performances in some churches (especially our living Christmas trees) competed favorably with many secular performances. You didn't have to be afraid of inviting your rich neighbors anymore to these productions. In fact, a few churches even named "producers" for their services, to coordinate all the setup, sound, lights, drama, music, sound tracks and most of all . . . the "flow." We searched for excellence and found it. In the last 15 years worship services in most churches — and all the growing ones — have gotten to be first class. These churches now offer a fast-paced production which snaps along as quickly as a TV special, and is almost as interesting.

One thing you've got to give us Boomers credit for — we do things well. We do not always see the implications of our revolutions, but the revolution itself is always done well. However, in this move to "production worship," what we did not count on was the eventual effect of our fast-paced, excellence-in-production-spectator orientation.

It took several years for our "customers" to notice it. But they eventually started to sense there was something missing. Our music now only expressed the "top half" of human religious emotion — the happy half. Our preaching eventually focused only on the sunny half of the gospel, and people increasingly sensed a part was missing from their diet. But most of all, our fast-paced, snappy services eventually left people feeling frantic and hurried, much like they feel on a busy freeway.

This is where an increasing number of lay worshipers are today. They think their worship service feels somehow "contrived" or unnatural, even "fake." They are tired of being spectators, of "watching" worship. They are weary of being shouted at — they want conversational preaching and a more subdued tone from the singers too. (You can shout at people in either music or preaching.) They are weary of being whipped up and yearn for a more peaceful, relaxed worship experience. "Mellow" may be the term. They are even willing to (EEEEEEK!) have times of "silence" (of the Quaker variety) as a part of the service. Some are even falling in love with the mournful, pensive saxophone sound in worship (thank you, Kenny). An increasing number of laity now want a worship service to reflect the "bottom half" of human religious emotion too . . . the half where mourning, brokenness, grieving, sorrow, pain and sadness are expressed.

How disappointing! Now that we've finally got it right, they aren't happy. What do they want? They want something more *real:* "I wish it was more authentic." What do they mean? They feel that what we have produced is "contrived," too perfect. Whaaaaat? Too perfect? How can that be? We have always assumed that perfection was exactly the goal of worship!

Consider Mariah Carey for example. Excellence-bent Boomers could not comprehend why she had background "hash" fed into her "Music Box" CD. (I have not met one Boomer yet who understands this . . . they just wag their heads and treat the news like purple hair — "Now why would they want to do that?") Why make anything less perfect? We were delighted to toss out our scratchy old LP records. Why feed background "hash" into a perfectly good CD recording? Because it sounds more "real" to a generation overdosed on perfect production. Increasingly, "authentic" is becoming more important than "perfection."

I saw this illustrated last month in a church that featured a trumpet solo by a mildly retarded young man. Along the way, he missed his tune and started playing several notes off. Boomers squirmed. You could tell they were worried about how visitors might perceive this imperfect performance. However, at lunch with several Generation X people, the remarks were totally different: "Wasn't that trumpet solo great . . . that's exactly what the real church should be!" The solo was "real." The "hash" didn't bother them, so long as it was "authentic." Now, I am not suggesting that we need to add more second-rate music. I'm a Boomer and I've had my share of it. The story, however, illustrates a growing desire out there for something more "real" in worship. We might call it "acoustic worship."

Several years ago MTV swept the market with its "unplugged" series. Why? Because it sounds so "real." Sure, there is still plenty of technical work in the background, but the acoustic sound itself is the real thing. This is the hunger I see among the laymen I talk to and get e-mail from. They are hungry for a fresh revolution in worship. They want a more "real" tone to worship. They thirst for the "real presence" of God, not just hype.

New trends begin with a hunger or desire. I wonder if this hunger will lead to a new movement toward "acoustic worship." I already see the beginnings of this revolution. Will it continue? Will we have worship that feels less contrived, less performance-oriented, less "put on" for the audience. Will we see the end of the spectator church? Some even predict a resurgence of classical liturgy, pageantry and creeds. Will we find a way to make worship feel more "real" and less "performed"? Is there a way to re-introduce in a fresh way testimonies, silence, brokenness-seeking elements. And perhaps the most disturbing question of all might be, "Will today's production churches be able to adapt to this trend?" Or will they stay stuck in the 1980s forever?

1. Have you seen any evidence of this "unplugged" trend or noticed a desire for "authentic," non-perfect music or services?

2. Some argue that every generation makes war with its parents and peace with its grandparents. What similarities do you see between this younger generation's interests and their second-world-war-era grandparents?

3. Whichever generation is in charge of worship styles is satisfied with the status quo and usually thinks there is too much emphasis on generational preferences in worship. Why would this be?

4. In what ways would you like to see a more "real" atmosphere in your church's worship?

5. In your opinion, what so-called "real" innovations seem to be merely an excuse for lack of excellence?

6. What would you say is the ratio of happy-upbeat to mournful-pensive music in the worship with which you are most familiar?

RELIGIOUS POSTUM

Experimenting in a horse barn with mixtures of molasses, bran and wheat 101 years ago, Charles William Post invented a coffee substitute which he humbly named after himself: "Postum." Americans had "coffee-free coffee." It tasted like the real thing, but with none of the caffeine risks. Sales zoomed, sparking Post to introduce a second brand of coffee substitute, which promptly flopped. So Post simply reintroduced the same stuff, this time as a cereal: Grape Nuts (which is neither, of course). What Post discovered with Postum was the American penchant for substitutes.

For the next 62 years many Postum drinkers sweetened their coffee-free coffee with good old-fashioned sugar. That is, until 1957 when Chevy made its best car and Americans welcomed a friendly little pink packet called "Sweet 'n Low." We now had sugar-free sugar. How about cream? You take cream? Well, perhaps you did until 1963, when we got cream-free cream in the form of the new "Cremora." Postum drinkers could now have their coffee-free coffee with cream-free cream and sugar-free sugar.

In the summer of 1969, as American youth thronged to Woodstock, New York, American business introduced a neat little jar which would delight salad lovers everywhere — bacon-free bacon: "Bac-O's." And 15 years ago, the 1980s brought even better news to sweetness-lovers with the introduction of a new sugar-free sugar that was actually sweeter than sugar: "NutraSweet." How's that! A substitute better than the real thing, and with none of the risks — tastes sweeter, but you don't get fat and lose all your teeth by age 50.

In 1995, while America was being hyped about the new Windows 95, the more important and lasting news was the quiet approval and introduction of "Olestra." Americans have arrived: we now have fat-free fat!

It appears that Americans like substitutes. Old-fashioned things like coffee, sugar, bacon-from-a-pig, cooking oil or lard are considered out of style and unhealthy. Many Americans actually prefer the substitute to the real thing, especially if there is anything disagreeable or risky in the real thing.

The question is, does this proclivity extend to our religion?

1. If there were a religion which "tasted" like the real thing but had no side effects, what would it look like?

2. What tendencies in our present forms of religion provide the "taste" of real religion without the costs or demands?

3. What are the dangers of substituting something else for the real thing in religion?

4. Where in the Bible do you recall an instance (actually several) where the people substituted a man-made religion for the real thing?

5. When a church finds itself involved in substitute religion, how can it get back to the real thing? What steps must it take?

6. What "side effects" of real religion do people sometimes want to escape?

WHAT REVIVAL? 32

American Christians love the idea of "revival." We like to imagine one is just around the corner and as soon as it gets here it will fix our crumbling spirituality and get the church back on track. Worse, our hope causes us to see revival mirages when there is nothing but desert before us. Nevertheless, expecting a revival is a popular American pastime. It fits our optimistic outlook. Many say we are in a great revival right now.

Are we? Is a revival happening right under our noses? What about Promise Keepers? Aren't these gatherings a sign of revival? Or, what about the quadrillion Super Churches we now have sprawling at the edges of every city? Or, how about all the emphasis on church planting? Aren't these signs of revival? What about the scores of preachers on TV — not to mention Dobson, Christian bookstores, the Church Growth movement, contemporary Christian music, holy laughter, Amway and the 700 Club. What more can I say? Certainly we must be right on the edge of the "Coming World Revival," right?

Sorry. If this is revival, then something's out of whack. What? If we're in a revival, how come it's not affecting church attendance. Consider Barna's findings. Only 37% of Americans say they've attended a religious service in the past week — down from 49% just five years ago. You read that right — a 12% decline since 1991! This is what the church growth experts call a "significant negative-growth rate." If it was happening in your church, you might be looking for another church. But when it happens across a whole nation you say, "the bottom's dropping out."

This is revival? If we were having a real revival, don't you think people would go to religious services more, not less? What kind of "revival" makes you attend church less? What we've had isn't real revival, but "revival hype." It is "virtual revival" — all the sensations of revival without any of the risk or the cost. Gee, and right after we redesigned the church to reach all the "seekers" we were told were interested. But where are they? Apparently not in church.

The greatest attendance collapse came among people age 69 and above (a whopping 21% free-fall since 1991!). And those 50-68 registered a 6% loss in the last five years. OK, maybe we kept the Boomers? Sorry, they dropped like flies after Yard Guard . . . down a colossal 19% in five years! In fact, the only age group which "held its own" was the 18-30 group — "Busters" or Xers — which experienced "just" a loss of one percent. When you figure the total, we net a 12% loss in five years. Now I know you can't identify revival with church attendance . . . but shouldn't there be some connection between going to church and a country having a revival? So, what do all these figures add up to? Not revival. What you've got to put in the "tally" column is a major national collapse in church attendance — in just five years.

Now I suppose some will say I shouldn't be giving this information out so freely, seeing that most Americans determine what is right by the polls. That is, when they hear that everybody else is dropping out of church — or at least attending less — they'll get on board the latest fad, the way they did when they were told that Boomers were coming back to church. Good point. However, *USA Today* published Barna's results, and having an even larger circulation than my writing, I figure the word is already out. Besides, there is something really serious here to think about. After all our redesigning of the church to reach more people, how come fewer people are going to church than before our redecoration?

What's going on here? Why are people dropping out? Are more people just coming less? Have we bargained away something vital in our effort to entertain the masses? In putting "Christian Commitment 101" on the lower shelf for the seekers, have we succeeded in making seekers out of our formerly committed people? Is it hard to keep them down on the [local church] farm after they've seen the big city [convention] lights? Why are we seemingly holding the "twenty-somethings"? What happened to the oldsters? Are Barna's figures screwy? Are people just more willing to honestly report their non-attendance? If so, why? What does all this mean . . . other than confirming the fact that we are not in a great revival right now?

1. Is revival ever a national event or is it more commonly localized?

2. While a national revival may or may not be occurring, there is clearly "revival" happening in some places . . . in local churches, segments of churches, and in individuals' lives. So, what is a "revival"? If your city were to have one, how would you know? What would stop? Start? How would things be different?

3. What connection does expecting a revival have with faith? That is, if we do not expect a revival, can we have one?

4. How does a revival happen? Is it purely a phenomenon which God alone sends, or are there things humans can do which will invariably "cause" a revival?

5. What do you know of revivals that have occurred down through history: the Wesleyan revival, the Welch revival, the first and second "Great Awakenings" in America, and others? What happened at these times that caused us — and even secular scholars — to call them "revivals"?

6. Where would you go in the Bible to see stories of a spiritual revival? What do these stories teach?

7. So, what do you think? Do you think your country is in a spiritual revival, or not?

NOT ME! I'M NOT GOING!

(TO THE ALTAR)

Pastors tell me things have changed when it comes to the traditional altar call. People just won't come to the altar like they used to . . . at least at the end of the service. Once the music starts and the invitation is given, they freeze. Why? I've seen it too. You can get people to go to the altar to pray about a personal need, for "help," or to have a "grand closing time as a church family," but to come forward to repent? That's a different story. Why? What are they thinking? I've asked around and collected people's opinions about altar calls. According to what I've heard, here's what people are really thinking when we ministers ask them to come forward:

1. This is none of your business.

Why do you want me to go up in front of all these people who don't really even know me? My religion is a personal relationship between God and me. Going to the altar makes it too public.

2. Going up there would be humiliating.

It's downright embarrassing to walk up there and kneel down as if I am some sort of awful sinner or something like that. I'm no worse than the rest of the people in here, maybe even a little bit better.

3. Who are you to judge me?

What right do you have to tell me I should come up there? You have your views and I have mine. The world would be a better place if we just accepted each other's different views and didn't judge.

4. I already went.

I really need help with this whole mess I am going through, but I already went up during the open altar time earlier in the service. I got help already.

5. I don't trust you.

I have no idea what you preachers do in secret. Maybe you are just like Jim Bakker or Jimmy Swaggart. I'm not so sure I want to bow down before a preacher. You look sincere, but who knows what you're really covering up?

6. Since when can people change in an instant?

The whole idea of going to the altar doesn't fit my therapeutic model of how people change. People change gradually over months or years. A Twelve-Steps group or a counselor can help. But I don't buy this quick fix of simply going up front for a prayer and, presto, you're changed in an instant. If you want to help me, forget this altar call and start a support group.

These kinds of thoughts pass through the minds of an increasing number of people when we give altar calls today.

Yet, many of us still give them. Why? Because people still come. It's amazing. In spite of the cultural bias against it, people still move out when an altar call is given. I am sometimes told, "these people here don't go to the altar." But when I open it up, they stream forward. Sure some come just to "get help." But many seem to be really seeking God's face. Since they keep coming, I keep inviting them.

But there is a deeper reason I still give altar calls. These reasons are more theological. I believe God created human beings with "free will," that is, the freedom to make personal decisions. In the Garden of Eden, Adam and Eve used their free wills to disobey God. Enter depravity. That is, the human will from then on has been depraved, or bent toward sin. Our depraved will, though still free, is biased against obedience. As Augustine observed, we may be free to choose right, but we seem freer to choose wrong. So with such a darkened nature, how could we ever find God? Enter God's grace — the grace which precedes conversion, enlightening and drawing our hearts toward Him. When we decide to come to God, we experience saving grace. God's plan of salvation includes a provision for each personal decision to believe, confess, repent and receive — all acts which spring from the will. The human will is critical for conversion. Though the decision does not save us, the decision is a critical part of our salvation. The will is also critical in our sanctification. God does not make us holy automatically and without our cooperation and submission. The sanctification of God's people involves commitment, surrender, consecration and seeking — again, all acts of the will. (The theological part is almost over . . . be patient.)

So why do I keep giving altar calls? Because in my preaching I keep calling for a decision. And the altar call is one good way to "put the question" for decision. The decision people make will be critical to the conversion of sinners and the sanctification of believers. So I keep preaching for a verdict and calling for decision. And the altar call still works (almost) everywhere I go.

Now, I know some of you are going to remind me that John Wesley never gave a public invitation for people to receive Christ, and the church got along pretty well for many years with baptism as the act of public confession. I also recognize that the American campmeeting style altar call is a relatively recent innovation, given 2000 years of Christian history. So I am not saying the public altar call is a sacred cow. I am suggesting, however, that it may have more life in it than we think. I'm all for burying all the smelly corpses lying around. But not while they're still breathing.

Sure, you can preach for a verdict and call for decision without giving an altar call. There are an increasing number of other "decision devices" which are working today. Some speakers who invite seekers to meet in a counseling room have good results. Others call on people to raise their hands or sign a card. More recently preachers invite those with spiritual needs to simply glance up and catch the speaker's eye. These methods are not wrong. In fact, as a guest speaker, I sometimes invite people to lift a hand to indicate to the pastor that they want an appointment to talk about spiritual things. And, I make sure the pastor makes a list. But I also still use a standard altar call. And believe it or not (given all the bias against it mentioned above), people often stream forward. So I still give altar calls. Before I toss out an old method, I want to make sure I have its underlying principle or doctrine embedded in the new method. I think the underlying principles here are to preach for a verdict, call for a decision, and avoid sermons which are pretty to listen to but never lead to a crisis decision of "what you will do with the man called Jesus."

1. Is the "altar call" as we have known it on the way out?

2. What kind of "invitation" do you prefer? If you were bringing an unbelieving friend to church, how would you want your church to invite this friend to repent and receive Christ?

3. If the church discards the actual practice of public altar calls, what kinds of public confession could replace them?

4. What are the advantages of a public altar call?

5. What are the chief disadvantages of public altar calls for people today?

6. Of those you know, how many were "saved" in a public altar call, and how many came to the point of faith in some other manner?

FIBERGLASS MINISTRY

Some time ago I got to take my family to the Old Town Canoe Factory in Maine. This company captured my heart 25 years ago, when I first watched line after line of remarkable craftsmen coax willful wood into the exquisite shapes of an Old Town design. I've always hungered to have one of those wonderful wood 'n canvas canoes — just to have it, even if I never used it much (like the piano my wife had for years).

I was determined to take my son to see these craftsmen. Boy, were we disappointed. The tour of the actual canoe-building shop has been replaced by a visitor center video presentation (a "virtual tour," I suppose). Of the 116 canoes on display, only two were wooden. Wood canoes are disappearing — too much time to make, too expensive to buy. It doesn't matter that they exhibit wonderful craftsmanship. Fiberglass is cheaper, lighter and more durable.

My romance with the Old Town Canoe Company ended. I couldn't even enjoy the craftsmanship of the two "real" canoes on display. They seemed out of place — like antiques — as if to say, "This is what we used to do . . . when canoes were real canoes . . . but we don't do much of this anymore."

I guess I really can't blame the Old Town Canoe Company for "following the market." After all, even the wood canoe replaced the birchbark canoe a hundred years before, because the wood canoe was cheaper and more durable. Now fiberglass replaces wood. Both canoes will get you over the water fine. And when I think of it, the Old Town Canoe Company's business is not essentially making canoes — it is making money. So they have to follow the market or go out of business. If they had kept on making only wood canoes, they would eventually wind up making canoes for only prayer-meeting-sized markets.

As I drove south, it occurred to me that this is what we sometimes do in the church. The market moves on us and we have to go along. Something faster, cheaper, better, lighter comes along, and we follow the market. Take preaching, for instance. Sermons that show the exquisite craftsmanship of two or three days of careful preparation are wood 'n canvas sermons. The beautiful craftsmanship of live storytelling is giving way to the fiberglass story — playing a video for the kids. Hard, sweaty research through hundreds of musty books in a "study" is wood 'n canvas preparation. It has given way to cassette-research and searching through CD-ROMs or the Internet. Pastoral calling eventually gives way to the faster, cheaper, more efficient method of midweek mailings. And there is not one of you who would really like to return to the "craftsmanship" of making those blue stencils for a mimeograph machine! We were as glad to take up the Xerox machines as the Native Americans were to toss aside their bows for rifles. Methods change.

However, I still love to see a beautiful wood canoe even though I can't afford to own one. I also still love to hear a wood 'n canvas sermon once in a while. Or hear a live storyteller. And, in spite of the plethora of stuff I can dig up on the Internet, I still love books. Perhaps it is part nostalgia and part appreciation for great craftsmanship. Either way, I still enjoy listening to a carefully crafted sermon once in a while. Even if I can't afford to own many myself.

1. Which of the changes we have made to worship, education, preaching, and the general program of the church do you consider more efficient yet also cause you to miss the "old way" a bit?

2. The element of "craftsmanship" is clear in canoe-making. But how does "craftsmanship" show itself in church work?

3. What real "craftsmen" or women do you look up to in the matter of spiritual craftsmanship?

4. What dangers are there in yearning for the "old ways," even if they were better? What effect can such yearning have on a person or church?

5. What methods (for church or personal spiritual growth) are not really changeable or easily made more "efficient," but must be done the "old way" to be effective? For instance, are there shortcuts or more efficient and faster ways to do prayer today than the "old way"?

6. What "old ways" of doing things (related to the church or personal spiritual life) are you quite happy to be rid of now?

7. Where would you go in the Bible to find an illustration of how old methods had to be discarded to make way for an improved channel to God? Where would you look to find an illustration of how "improvements" weren't really improvements at all, but sidetracks from real religion?

IS BEING A PASTOR HARDER TODAY?

There seem to be a lot of churches anxious to dump their pastors. An almost-equal number of pastors confess to being "half-burned out" and are looking for a way of escape. Perhaps I'm hearing about the worst cases, but it sure looks like pastoring is tougher than it was forty years ago. My pastor-father pretty much always expected a "unanimous vote." To him, a few "no votes" meant it was time to move on. Not so today. Pastors simply expect some opposition as part of the "cost of doing business." What has changed? Why are church members more willing to criticize, oppose or vote against a pastor today?

1. Loss of spiritual respect.

Thirty years ago my pastor-father's primary job was to pray, call on people, study and preach. The pastor was considered "godly," and even respectfully called "Preacher" or "Reverend." My dad pastored the largest church in his area, but he didn't even have an office in the church. He had a "study" at home, and that's what he did there — study. When people in town discovered that he was a minister, they responded with an almost hushed respect — and often with a discount! Not so today in the post-Swaggart/Bakker era. Now that the general opinion of the profession has sunk closer to the media, congressmen and lawyers, many ministers hide their identities.

But we haven't just lost this spiritual aura in the world; it's dimmed in the church too. I sometimes wonder if this is because of the change in what we actually do now. Today's busy pastor has more in common with a YMCA director or business manager than the preacher of the 1950s. Many of today's church offices hum like an insurance agency, complete with a photocopy machine, computer, office hours and a paid secretary. The work of a pastor has changed from praying, calling, study, reading and sermon preparation to leadership and managerial activities related to a sprawling church-activities calendar. Laity increasingly view ministers as employed "program managers" or "church administrators" more than as "prophets of God." Does this make them more comfortable criticizing our productivity, or "firing a non-producer"? Have we brought some of this on ourselves?

We ministers now swim with all the other management sharks — and sometimes pay the same price for it. Many laymen on the board are better experts than the pastor at these things, and we sometimes look bad, in spite of our decade's reading of management books. Seldom does a pastor get the boot for being a poor preacher or weak in fasting, but more often it is because he is a "weak leader" or "poor administrator." Many pastors are totally out of their areas of expertise. Certainly we can't turn back the clock. But has this massive change in the nature of our work gotten us into situations for which we have little or no seminary training, and eventually made us less effective at doing what we were not trained to do? Hmmmmmmmmmm . . .

2. Increasing expectations.

People's expectations have changed too. Members today expect excellence, quality — even perfection. A pastor should be likable, funny, a good organizer, great office manager, have excellent people skills, have good-looking, well-behaved kids, stay slim, dress well, be a "good communicator," and be willing to work for considerably less than some of the board members. Anything less, and some members get dissatisfied. The trouble is, we ministers aren't perfect. (Neither is Robert Schuller if you had the chance to be around him all week.) People expect more today. And when they don't get it, they are willing to oppose the pastor, maybe even try to "run 'em off." A pastor needs to be better today — just to survive. If you aren't really good, you might not "make the cut" with some people. It's hard to be perfect when you're not.

3. Too much change.

Many pastors get ousted because they "made too many changes too fast." Right now we are going through a period of massive change in worship styles. The wise old-timers always said, "You can change a lot of things, but when you mess with the worship style you're asking for trouble." Well, we've been messing with the morning worship service a lot during these last ten years. And lots of people don't like it. Some of them are willing to get even. They don't like the fact that you've changed what they've done in worship for a thousand years (actually it's only been 15 years, they just think their style is permanent). Today's consumer-member knows what flavor ice cream he or she wants, and if you can't serve that flavor, down the street they'll go . . . or, more likely, down the street you'll go. We are seeing a lot of this unrest because we have introduced too much change too fast.

4. The carnality factor.

Sure, we've always had carnal church members. And I know some people think the level of godliness is at an all-time high in the church. I don't. So, I suspect that the general level of spiritual shallowness and worldliness in the church has produced a good crop of the quack grass of carnality. And it's not all lay-carnality either.

5. The "Moral Majority" factor.

I know, Jerry Falwell's "Moral Majority" evaporated long ago. But the Moral Majority mothered a dozen other movements committed to changing society. For more than a decade, Evangelicals have trained our people in the fine art of how to get your own way. We've taught our people to use war terminology, power tactics, and organized protests to attack the enemy. We've trained members to organize, sign petitions, boycott products, write congressmen, protest, organize, and wield power to get what they want. Could it be that they've learned the lesson too well? Is it possible we didn't recognize that we were teaching them a *method* of getting what they want? And now this dog has turned and bit us in the rear end? I fear that many churches have gotten better at effecting change through petitions, protest letters, and power blocks than by engagement, discussion, compromise and prayer. Are we now more at home with boycotts than the Bible? At organizing a "no" vote than organizing a VBS?

I hope not. But from what I hear through regular contact with pastors, there is a tremendous amount of turmoil in local churches. Not everywhere, mind you. But it will take a considerable amount of evidence to persuade me that pastoring is not harder today than it was forty years ago.

But then again, if today's ministry is harder, God certainly wouldn't leave us high and dry, would He? Won't He supply increasing grace to handle it? "He giveth more grace when the burdens grow greater . . ."

Is ministry today more difficult than 40 years ago? Is it easier? In what ways?

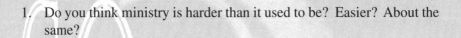

1. Do you think ministry is harder than it used to be? Easier? About the same?

2. Are people more willing to criticize ministers today than they used to be? Why? Do ministers deserve it more?

3. What do you think about the shift from "Preacher" to CEO among many ministers today? Is it a good change or not? Necessary or a mistake?

4. If the ministry is so hard, even harder than ever, how come so many "preachers' kids" still go into the ministry? How do you account for this?

5. Is it harder to be a *Christian* today than it was 40 years ago? Easier? Why?

6. What are the common difficulties of a minister's life at times? What are the common advantages in all times?

7. What are the kinds of things your church might do — or you personally might do — to encourage your minister?

GUTSY MINISTRY

The ministry today is no job for the weak. It takes guts. I want to pay tribute to the gutsy ministers I know — those who swim upstream against the prevailing culture, who pay the price for maintaining a solid ministry to a generation in love with whipped cream.

1. In a day when easy-believism prevails, some ministers insist that Christian conversion should actually change lives and make people different. That takes guts.

2. In a day when the prevailing conversion models are largely gradual and additive ("accepting Christ," "starting new" or "receiving Christ"), some ministers have the guts to preach repentance and a decisive turning away from sin.

3. In a day when many "evangelical" churches flatter people — approving and excusing all kinds of sin so long as they keep coming — some of you have the guts to tell your own church folk they're sub-Christian, then watch them cross town to be approved elsewhere. Whew!

4. In a day when the only thing you can be legalistic about is anti-legalism, some ministers have the guts to caution church members about the hazards of TV, movies, videos, CATV and the Internet.

5. In a day when the only acceptable view of God among Evangelicals is a soft, tender, understanding Mister Rogers-in-the-Sky, some ministers have the guts to remind people of "the other face of God" — His stern, wrathful, judgment side which hates and punishes sin.

6. In a day when people can get uplifting, cheery, feel-good, pop psychology from a smooth-talking "communicator" across town, some of you have the guts to preach deep theological truth that requires hard chewing on the part of your listeners.

7. In a day when the accepted fad is to concentrate primarily on felt needs, when most people pick a church based on these need-meeting services, some ministers have the guts to purposely design church services to meet God's needs (and the actual deepest [spiritual] need of people).

8. In a day when the worst cultural sin is "intolerance," a lack of sympathy for "victims," some ministers have the guts to preach about sin — calling sin, sin — actually naming it, condemning certain behaviors and attitudes, and quoting from the Bible.

9. In a day when the sacred is trivialized and the holy is treated lightly, some ministers have the guts to elevate the sacraments, insisting on a more frequent coming to the Lord's Table.

10. In a day when entry level religion has become the norm and most folk believe God marks on a curve, some ministers have the guts to expect Christians to abandon self-centeredness, straighten up and live right, begin tithing, and attend church more than an hour a week.

11. In a day when religion has been privatized and it is difficult to coax seekers to even glance up and nod as a sign of their spiritual need, some ministers have the guts to issue calls for decision, even encouraging people to walk out to the altar in front of the entire crowd! How do you do that?

12. In a day when interest-driven studies and accommodating "felt needs" are the pattern, some ministers have the guts to insist on the Bible as the primary text in Sunday school and small groups. Amazing!

13. In a day when thousands of evangelical churches will take just about anyone who walks by into membership, some ministers have the guts to tell prospective members to wait a while yet before joining your church. Whew!

14. In a day when vast numbers of Evangelicals have fallen head-over-heels in love with modernity, some ministers have the guts to call for separation from and non-conformity to worldliness and a worldly mind-set.

15. In a day when shallow, universalistic, bloodless, generalized choruses are the only "politically correct" music, some ministers have the guts to insist on including music with the deeper themes of Scripture. How do you survive?

16. In a day of pragmatism, when doing "what works" is still the route to fame and money for an evangelical pastor, some ministers have the guts to make ministry decisions which fly in the face of conventional wisdom — just because of your convictions.

17. In a day of therapeutic preaching, smoothing over sin and general "Phil Donahuism," some ministers have the guts to tell adulterous church members to stop it. What gall!

18. In a day when most people want affirmation and encouragement while they continue to live like they always have, some ministers have the guts to preach on the holiness of God and proclaim His call for the church to be a holy people. Whew!

19. In a day when most religious consumers want a sentimental, nearby, immanent helper-God who will enable them to become self-actualized, holistic, successful human beings, some ministers have the guts to proclaim a majestic, holy, all-powerful, transcendent God more concerned with justice and righteousness than finding His children parking spaces at the mall on rainy days.

20. In a day when some gleefully criticize the pastor, sign petitions against new ideas, form protest groups and power blocks, use the phone to recruit votes, and generally make their pastor's life miserable, some ministers have the guts to persist and stick with it . . . you "keep on keeping on," despite the pressures on you. What guts!

I admire gutsy pastors. Most pastors have enough guts to do some of these things. And some ministers have enough guts to do many of them. A few have enough guts to practice all of them (of course some of those will be looking for a new church soon). But whatever you think of the individual issues, you've got to admire gutsy ministers. I wonder sometimes if many laymen and women would actually like to have a more gutsy minister.

1. Which one of these twenty gutsy things do you think is the hardest for a minister to do?

2. Churches aren't really as hard on their pastors as this chapter seems to state. This is a collection of incidents from all across North America and doesn't represent one particular church (we hope!). However, which of these gutsy things characterizes your own minister? Do you respect him or her for it?

3. What gutsy actions and policies did the writer of this essay leave out? How have you seen guts demonstrated in a minister?

4. Leaving the matter of ministerial guts for the moment, what "takes guts" as a layman or woman today?

5. What incidents from the Bible portray people having the guts to do what was right despite the cost?

LISTENING TO OUR CRITICS

It is a lot easier to criticize than to be criticized. Most of us think it is inappropriate to be criticized by people under us, but we think the people over us deserve a bit of it. In the local church we see ourselves as Moses, and our critics as the grumbling people (Numbers 21). But when it comes to those in authority over us, we see ourselves as the Apostle Paul, and our leader as the Apostle Peter who needs a good rebuke and correction (Galatians 2). We often see the critics under us as carnal and negative, while we pronounce our criticism of those over us as informative, corrective, or an expression of our personal opinion. Face it, when it comes to criticism, most of us are better at dishing it out than taking it.

In fact, we ministers sometimes call criticism "sin." It sure seems sinful. Perhaps we do this because we associate criticism with the people who seem so gifted at doing it. They seem . . . well . . . they seem so "carnal." We say to ourselves "consider the source" and dismiss whatever they say. We assume these critics are bad people with bad motives. Sometimes they are. Maybe even often. So we dismiss whatever they say as "stinkin' thinkin'." We reject the messenger and we also reject the message. In doing so, however, we cut ourselves off from an opportunity to grow. Refusing to hear criticism (or hearing it only from those we like and respect), sets a time bomb ticking in our ministry. It may not go off for many years. But eventually it will go off. The point of this essay is that we should at least hear our critics. Hearing our critics today just might save us tomorrow.

Lay aside personal criticism for a while. Movements have critics too. It is even harder for a movement to hear its critics. Movements have a herd mentality — "If all these people think like me we must be right." In America "might makes right." The majority rules. If enough of us all head one way, we just assume that we are headed in the right direction. (We forget that the Gadarene swine were also in good formation, had good unity, and were all headed the same way.)

Movements don't have to hear their critics, especially in the early stages. The Spirit is moving. Growth is explosive. Success is sure. People are being ministered to. It is so easy to say, "This is of the Spirit, don't criticize." Movements (in their early stages) can simply steamroll right over their critics. And they can get away with it . . . for a while. But this refusal to self-examine will eventually cause the movement to self-destruct.

Consider the movement I am in — the "holiness movement." This movement was criticized in its early stages for several things, but the movement's proponents didn't need to listen. They could steamroll the critics. And they did. They were too successful to listen. People were getting saved by the tens of thousands. New churches sprouted up every week along with new colleges/Bible schools, para-church organizations, publishing houses, and even entire denominations. Gigantic gatherings of thousands of people flocked to campmeetings — sometimes larger gatherings than any secular gathering in the area. Campmeetings even started charging "gate fees" to attendees and thousands coughed up the cash without complaint. The "evangelists" were famous and powerful communicators. They held their audience "in the palm of their hand." When you have this much success, you don't need to listen to your critics.

But there were critics anyway. For instance, from the start in the holiness movement there was criticism of the movement's tendency toward emotionalism ("getting blessed," or "running the aisles," or "shouting"). Some critics warned that there was too much emphasis on instantaneous sanctification and not enough on the gradual or progressive side. Others criticized the tendency toward legalism. But in the heady early days of a movement — when thousands of people are caught up in the excitement — a movement can roll right over its critics, ignoring them completely. For a time.

Or consider a more recent movement — the "church growth movement." In the 1970s critics warned of an overemphasis on numbers and where that might lead us. They were stomped down with such phrases as, "The people who don't want to talk about numbers don't have any." Other critics warned that there appeared to be an anti-education bias, but they were steamrolled with, "Those who can do, those who can't, teach." Still other critics raised concern about adapting the church too much to market principles. They were overrun with, "But it works — look at all the people coming now." The critics of the church growth movement — when it was on the upswing — were dismissed as "losers" and whiners.

Now that the church growth Supernova has collapsed in on itself, many of us wish we'd listened more carefully to these early critics. They may have been half wrong. But they may have been half right too.

Enough about movements. Back to the critics we face personally. That's more practical. What should we do with personal criticism? Not just ministers, but church boards or leaders in general. What should we do?

1. Invite it through evaluation.

Some people don't need an evaluation form; they are simply critical by nature. But most people seldom offer criticism (to you) unless they have a safe way to do it. Using a feedback form a few times will get most of us all the criticism we need (or can handle). A sheet like this gives the entire congregation a chance for input, not just the outspoken ones. And sometimes this input puts the hyper-critical people in their place — reminding them how poorly they represent the whole congregation. But at other times, the collected input may agree exactly with what the outspoken critics have been saying all along. (This is the time to eat humble pie.) The best feedback forms are simple and include only a few questions: (1) What are we doing that is GOOD and should keep doing? (2) What are we doing that we ought to CHANGE? (3) What are we not doing that we should START? So, ask for criticism and get it from the whole church.

2. Look for the grain of truth.

While we might resent or reject our critics, there is often a grain of truth in what they say. We should ask how much is true. 50%? 25%? 10%? Only 1%? Critics don't have to be completely right to be helpful. In fact, the majority of criticism may be "mostly wrong." But somewhere among the false criticism there is often a grain of truth. Ignoring this grain of truth would be like dismissing small concentrations of lead in our water supply. Eventually the little grains pile up and poison a person's effectiveness.

For instance when I was developing Bible study curriculum in my work, getting criticism became a way of life for me. I sometimes got angry tirades blasting me for using the NIV version of the Bible. I personally favored the NIV over the KJV, so I was tempted to simply dismiss such criticism. However, when I looked for the grain of truth, I wound up seeing dedicated saints who had read "the Bible" for years — the only Bible they knew. Then along came this whippersnapper, who tore their familiar Scripture out of their hands and replaced it with new

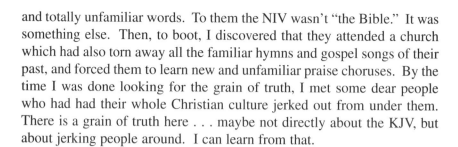
and totally unfamiliar words. To them the NIV wasn't "the Bible." It was something else. Then, to boot, I discovered that they attended a church which had also torn away all the familiar hymns and gospel songs of their past, and forced them to learn new and unfamiliar praise choruses. By the time I was done looking for the grain of truth, I met some dear people who had had their whole Christian culture jerked out from under them. There is a grain of truth here . . . maybe not directly about the KJV, but about jerking people around. I can learn from that.

3.   When they are 100% wrong, look at least for a valid warning.

Sometimes you can't find even 1% truth in criticism. It is flat out wrong. You are "falsely accused." But you can almost always find a "warning." Ask yourself, "What are they afraid of?" Even when the criticism is invalid, sometimes their fear is sound. For instance, a while ago a layman from Wisconsin circulated a series of letters accusing the Bible study curriculum I produce of being "soft on homosexuality." There was 0% truth in the accusation. We had run an article that said something like "the church should try to get homosexuals saved and delivered from sin." He perceived this as too soft.

However, even though there was not one grain of truth in the criticism, there was a good warning there. What was his fear? That the church would come to accept homosexual behavior as normal? Not a bad fear; in fact, a good warning. In the last few decades the church has adapted to all kinds of behavior the Bible condemns. (For instance, who of us would have imagined 25 years ago how quickly the church would come to accept divorce?) Could we adapt to homosexual behavior in the next 25 years? I hope not, but it is a worthy fear . . . and a warning. So even when there's not a grain of truth in what a critic says, the Lord can at least help us accept a good warning. It is one of the ways God uses our critics to make us smarter and better.

Sure, none of us enjoys listening to our critics. We'd rather just steamroll right over them, crushing their criticism into dust. However, listening to them today, just might save us in the future.

1. It is obvious that none of us likes to be criticized . . . but why is that? Why do we hate it so? What makes us resist criticism and consider it an attack?

2. Can a person listen too much to the critics? If so, what is the effect of this?

3. What are the practical ways a church can collect criticism from people — provide a "pop-off valve" — and at the same time keep in touch with what people are thinking?

4. How does all this apply to the family? How can you collect criticism at home — from your spouse or children — without giving up authority or getting shot down so badly that you want to give up?

5. Think theologically for a moment. If a person resists being criticized, what kind of inner doctrine drives this resistance? What does he really believe about himself that would make him refuse to receive criticism? Switch sides now; what doctrine or belief drives a person to be open to criticism?

6. Think of an incident in the Bible where someone offered constructive criticism to another and it paid off. Think of a time when the criticism was wrong and the person should have kept his/her mouth shut?

MULTILEVEL TITHING

The stewardship committee at my church has hatched a brilliant plan to end all our financial problems. I hope you'll join us, for it could make you personally rich, too. We think the Lord must have given us this plan, because it is a win-win situation . . . our church gets all the money it needs while, at the same time, our members get rich.

We call our new system the "give-and-it-shall-be-given-unto-you" campaign. It is simple and beautiful. You've heard of the idea of "tithing" I'm sure. It's the notion of giving 10% of your net income to the church. Sure, that sounds high at first, but what if you could get more than ten times that amount back — and keep getting it for years in the future? Sounds too good to be true, but think of all the things your family could use. That's where multilevel tithing comes in.

Here's how it works. Besides tithing yourself, our stewardship committee is prepared to pay you a premium of 10% of net income from every tither you personally recruit. And, we'll keep paying that 10% as long as they keep tithing. That could produce a reliable revenue stream for your family for decades!

For instance, if you recruit a tither who makes $50,000 a year, he or she will tithe $5,000. This means you get $500 as your 10% "finder's fee" — and you keep on getting that 10% every year your recruit keeps tithing! And when your recruit raises his or her giving (including missions pledges), you get a raise too. (See how this will add up to big bucks over the next decade?)

But it doesn't stop here. It is a multilevel system, meaning you also get a cut of the tithe from all those your recruits recruit too! This means that, besides the 10% fee from your own recruits, our stewardship committee will pay you a 2.5% fee — for every tither your recruits get on board! We believe, "it's better to teach a person to fish, than give them a fish." Or, in our case, "it's better to make a person a recruiter of tithers than just a tither." This means you not only get $500 a year from a $5,000 tither, but you will receive another $250 a year from any $5,000 tithers your recruit recruits. Nifty, huh?

But hold on to your chair, it gets even better! In order to motivate our tither-recruits to "go deep" in the multilevel approach, our stewardship committee will pay a full 20% — yes, that's a double rate! — on all third-level tithers your stewardship ministry produces: That's $1000 on any third-level $5,000 givers, plus the combined $750 from the first two levels producing a $1,750 total for recruiting three deep! You can readily see how important it is to not only recruit tithers, but to recruit tither-recruiters! With just a little work in the evenings and on weekends, you could be pulling down six figures a year, all while you are doing the Lord's work! And don't worry about the "cost" of all this to our church. The whole program only "costs" us a small part of our new income, low by any fund-raising standards and, after all, we wouldn't be getting this money anyway if you weren't recruiting new tithers — it's all new money. And the stewardship committee knows one more thing . . . of course you'll be paying tithe on this new income, so the church wins out on that too.

I'm sure after hearing about this plan, you'll want to sign up right away. Of course, the sooner you get on board, the faster you'll start getting those nice monthly checks — and the Lord's work will be benefiting. All I ask you to do is remember to write my name on your sign-up card (so I can get credit for recruiting you).

I'm just kidding, of course. This is all tongue-in-cheek satire, but it should provoke some thoughts anyway.

1. Forget the matter of stewardship for a moment and focus on all the multilevel schemes so prevalent in the evangelical church. How should the church deal with multilevel recruiters? Is it OK for multilevel folk to recruit others through the church? Classes? Small groups? What about the pastor using a board meeting to make a presentation? Where should a church draw the line on multilevel recruiting?

2. Now, to the matter of stewardship. Why is it that the church is so hungry for new schemes to finance its work? (When this essay first appeared on the Internet, scores of readers missed the satire and wrote in for a packet or for more information on how they could implement the plan in their church!) What drives this quest for an easier way to raise money in the church?

3. This satirical piece pokes fun at the idea of getting a kickback for tithing, but are there other ways people can give to their church and get direct personal benefit from their giving? Think a bit, there are plenty (many of them illegal, but the tax man has a hard time catching such schemes in the church).

4. What do you personally think is the best and simplest way to finance the church? How would you do it?

5. To what Scripture would you go to argue for a church financing plan? What does the Bible say?

SUCCESSFUL FAILURE

(NINE LESSONS WE CAN LEARN FROM FAILURE)

I've had plenty of success in my ministry "career." Probably too much, for my own good. But I've had a few whopping failures too, one of them being a six-year stint at headquarters attempting to resurrect my denomination's Sunday schools. All failure is not a loss, however. Even failures can be successful, if we learn from them. What are the lessons failure can teach us?

1. It reminds us of our limitations.

Failure shows us we're not invincible after all. It purges personal pride. Crucifies arrogance. Success teaches us to rely on ourselves and to trust our own cleverness; failure instructs is to rely more on God.

2. Failure helps us empathize.

A leader who never fails comes to dismiss unsuccessful people as lazy, stupid, or just plain "losers." Once you've laid an egg or two yourself, you have more empathy for other people's blunders.

3. Failure teaches us about timing.

Sometimes our timing is off. I learned this several years ago when I launched a massive program to persuade my entire denomination to unplug their TV sets during the first week of January. Encouraging them to spend more time with family, read the Bible and pray, sounded like a brilliant idea to me. But it fell flat on its face. Not just because of the playoffs (though that was a timing factor too), but for another reason. My denomination still has a lot of refugees from legalism. They wanted nothing whatsoever to do with unplugging their TVs — the whole idea sounded like we were turning back the clock. So it flopped. But in the years since, several totally secular movements with the same goal have achieved grand success. I suppose with such secular support the idea might fly today. My timing was off. I've seen pastors' ideas on building programs or additional staff voted down. Sometimes we try to do the right thing at the wrong time, so we fail.

4. Failure teaches us to see the parts, not just the whole.

When the whole enchilada is going up in smoke, we learn to look for little successes within the larger failure — people we have ministered to, lives which have been changed, prayers that have been answered, the early signs of a turnaround. And, after all, when we all finally retire and review our life of ministry, we'll not remember the big successes anyway. We'll remember the individual people down through the years whose lives we helped to change.

5. Some failures happen because of the size of the task.

Some goals will never achieve total success: "Winning the world to Jesus"; "Discipling people to perfect Christ-likeness"; "Developing a well-trained ministry." Yet these tasks are worthwhile anyway. In fact, perhaps they are worthwhile *because* they are too big to accomplish. With such tasks, the romance is in the effort, not the achievement. More important than our failure may be determining what we failed trying to do.

6. Failure can tell us we've got the wrong job.

There's such a thing as a "person-job match" or a "pastor-church match." Some jobs don't fit some leaders. Some leaders, who would do quite well somewhere else, flop where they are. It's a "bad fit." Sometimes we have to fail at one place so we can leave and succeed somewhere else. Our successor may succeed where we have failed . . . not because he is better, but because he is different. He "fits" better. And so do you, now.

7. Failure reminds us of the "Nazareth Principle."

Face it, there are some churches Jesus himself couldn't resurrect. Causes, too.

8. Failure reminds us of the Kingdom's seasonal nature.

Taking in a grand harvest is the most "successful" work of all. But sometimes we are on duty when harvesting is "out of season." What then? We must "be instant in season, out of season" (2 Tim. 4:2 KJV). Sometimes God uses one leader to plant a crop, or prepare the soil, or do the watering, but it will be a later pastor or leader who gets to reap the harvest. Our "failure" is really a stage in the cycle.

9. Failure reminds us of our faulty definition of success.

How is "success" defined in the church? The same way it's defined in the world: numbers, money, fame. And, though we deny having these values, most of us still live by them, or at least keep our eye on them. However, when you experience failure, God's corrective definition of success (eventually) looms much larger. And His definition is the only one which counts.

1. Have you ever failed? Tell someone about it. What did you learn from it?

2. Some argue that men or women will never be fully trusted as leaders unless they have first had a major failure in their lives. Why do you think people say this? Do you agree?

3. What happens when a person refuses to learn from failures? What is the alternative?

4. Can you cite "failures" in the Bible which were not failures at all in God's eyes, though in human terms they seemed to be big flops?

5. What stories from the Bible or history can you give to illustrate how a failure can be the foundation for later achievement?

6. The old motto says, "Jesus never fails." Yet He was perceived to have failed at times. When? What lesson can we learn from Jesus himself about failure?

40 BLUE MONDAYS

Most pastors know what you're talking about when you say "Blue Monday." They've had them. Maybe often. Blue Monday is more than a Monday morning hangover. It's closer to a feeling of failure — wanting to give up and walk away. Usually by the middle of the week the gloom lifts and you are back to your old self. But not always. The pastors I talk with can often name what triggered their Blue Monday. If these stories sound true, it is because they are:

After several years of prayerful planning and with the unanimous support of the board, you bring your relocation plans before the church. It does not pass.

You persuade your mentor to be the guest speaker for a Saturday night marriage seminar. A few older ladies show up — all widows. You discover Sunday morning that your younger couples went as a group to a hockey game.

You preach a powerful sermon on the Lord's will and sense God's anointing. The biggest response you get is from a member who corrects your pronunciation of Phrygia.

Yesterday was your farewell Sunday. After pastoring the same church for 30 years, leading from zero to 900, they gave you a clock.

You gradually become convinced that what your people really want are general sermons that encourage and entertain, not specific sermons that convict and challenge. You are tempted to give them what they want.

Your Treasurer tells you that they can no longer afford to pay your family's insurance because they need to build up the church's Rainy Day Fund.

You preached your heart out yesterday — after an almost sleepless night burdened with your congregation's spiritual poverty. Your people sat like gravestones during the service. Those who needed the message most nodded off to sleep several times.

You lead a dozen people for over a month in preparation for yesterday's big attendance drive. Once the results are in, you total an increase of exactly five from the Sunday before.

After thinking over this week's board meeting for several days, you conclude that this church really wants a YMCA director to coordinate all the programs, and not a pastor-teacher like you've trained to be.

You write a check to the plumber for five hours' work. It is more than your whole week's paycheck.

You gave your fifteenth consecutive altar call yesterday — to which nobody responded.

Almost everybody responded to your invitation to seek racial reconciliation last month. It occurs to you today that nobody did anything more about it.

The people clearly like your assistant pastor much more than you.

Yesterday your senior pastor told you that you don't work hard enough.

You read in your denominational paper this morning that the only pastors who get praise are those whose churches are "Fast-Growing." Yours isn't even growing slowly.

The major employer in your town laid off 200-300 people last month. Every second week another couple tells you they'll be moving out of town.

The Treasurer tells you after service that the giving has been slipping over the last few months because several key members seem to be withholding their tithes for some reason or another.

As your people left the church yesterday, they didn't seem to notice that you had preached.

You wonder if both you and the church are just going through the motions — this doesn't seem to be the real thing.

Most pastors, like parents, have had a Blue Monday triggered by something like the above. It tempts them to just give up sometimes — toss in the towel and walk away. They seldom do, but they sometimes feel like it just the same. Though most pastors keep a joyful spirit before their people (they have to!), the most common emotion they share with their friends in confidence is discouragement.

But the question isn't why pastors feel this way on some Mondays. The question is, why do they stick in there anyway — even through a string of Blue Mondays? Why would a pastor still keep on keeping on?

Is it the money? Fame? Personal satisfaction? Just for the fun of it? I don't think so.

I think it has something to do with *the call*. *The call* takes you through Blue Mondays . . . even Blue Februarys. Those who do ministry for fun, or money, or a nice career, or because their grandmother prayed them into it, don't make it through Blue Mondays. They'd rather hang drywall, or be a security guard. I think it's *the call*.

1. Do you think pastors have more to get discouraged about than any other person? Don't most people at times feel like they want to give up? Are pastors any different? Why or why not?

2. What is *the call* to ministry in your mind? Is it any different than any other person's career choice? How?

3. In the real life examples given above, which do you think are trivial and should have been dismissed by the pastor? Which do you think are serious issues and need to be addressed or corrected (if you were able to remedy the situation)?

4. What physical, emotional and psychological factors do you think creep into the life of a minister — on Mondays particularly?

5. What kinds of things sometimes cause the laity to have similar "Blue Mondays" about their church?

6. What practical things can a church member do to help a minister through times like "Blue Mondays"?

7. Who in the Bible illustrates this kind of discouragement in the Lord's work?

ARE YOU DISCIPLING YOUR OWN KIDS?

The answer is yes. Discipling our children is not optional. If you have kids (or grandkids), you *are* discipling them. You might be discipling them for good or bad, but you are discipling them. There are at least four ways parents disciple their kids:

1. Accidental Discipleship.

Discipling is not always purposeful. Sometimes we disciple our children without them or us knowing it. For instance, I remember as a little boy hanging around my dad during a work day at camp. During a coffee break, a knot of guys told an off-color joke. I noticed that my father didn't join the guffaws. I watched him gently shift the conversation to a higher level. He was discipling me . . . accidentally. You and I have all kinds of opportunities like this to disciple our kids accidentally. "More is caught than taught."

2. Discipleship Moments.

Have you had moments when your child is especially open to you? You know, those half-minute windows when they are approachable? These are Discipleship moments and kids are open for influence . . . even if only for a moment. I remember discovering an item in my mother's grocery sack for which a clerk had forgotten to charge my mother. She said, "We could keep this and they would never know, but that would be wrong." She sent me back with the exact change. My mother was discipling me in integrity with that short sentence. We did a lot of discipleship with my own kids while we watched television. When we saw something contrary to Christian values, we often made corrective comments. Just for the moment. This is discipleship, too.

3. Discipleship Events.

Great celebration events have a major impact on kids. Consider the feasts and holy days of Old Testament times. These were perhaps the primary means of discipling Jewish children. Children love big events. For years my family got up at 4:00 a.m. on Easter to attend a citywide Easter pageant. It was a purposeful annual event designed to disciple my kids. When my sons were little kids, I promised them I'd take them on a father-son tour of Israel when they turned 12. They remembered. I had to keep my promise. It was a monumental spiritual event in the lives of both sons. This is Event discipleship and our busy lives don't allow enough of it.

4. Scheduled Discipleship.

This is what we think of mostly when we hear the word "Discipleship." It is meeting with your child on a scheduled basis and working through a Bible book or discipleship materials. The old-fashioned family devotions were "scheduled discipleship," though so few Christian families do that anymore. If you don't do family devotions, what have you replaced them with? I know one father who got up every morning for Bible study with his son for two years straight. I talked with a mother who met for a half hour after school three days a week with her daughter. When each of my sons turned twelve, I started taking them to a restaurant for a Discipleship Breakfast one day a week for two or three years. We studied verse by verse through Matthew, then Acts. We went through a couple of other discipleship books. We had fun. We just talked. I remember overhearing one of my sons talking about discipleship with another teen. He said, "My Dad discipled me." He wasn't talking about the more important means of discipleship — the informal, unscheduled and often accidental kinds of discipleship. He was speaking of the formal breakfast times together. That's the advantage of scheduled discipleship — the child knows it and feels discipled.

Do you have kids at home? Grandkids nearby? Perhaps you need to think about adding some sort of formal, scheduled discipleship for your child or grandchild? Family devotions? A discipleship breakfast?

Sunday breakfast? After school? If so, don't delay too long. A lot of the other things you plan to do this year can be done even after the kids leave for college. But the window of opportunity to disciple your own kids closes fast. Faster than you'd think.

1. Tell how somebody "discipled" you "accidentally" and informally?

2. What does "discipleship" actually mean? What are you trying to see happen in another person when you "disciple"? What is the difference between discipling and teaching?

3. What other formal or scheduled ways have you heard of people discipling their children?

4. Can you disciple somebody who is not a convert?

5. Is a person ever completely "discipled"? Is there an end to discipling or does it last forever?

6. What Bible examples of discipleship can you offer to illustrate discipleship of others, especially children?

THE COLLAPSE OF EGO-BASED MINISTRY

S omething's switched in this last few years or so across the church. The "Big Ego Style" of ministry is out. It has collapsed. I don't know why for sure. Perhaps it has just run its course. Or the change may be driven by the Generation X penchant for making ordinary people their heroes. But for whatever reason, ego-based ministry is a thing of the past.

I see it in conversations with district or conference leaders: "I don't want a hotshot, shooting-star type — I want a quality guy who will stick by the stuff and do what's right." I see it in senior pastors talking about staff openings: "I don't want a "pied piper" that is all personality — I want a solid fellow who will stick to the basics and build the kids, not his own fame." The words I hear increasingly are "solid," "quality guy," "reliable," "integrity" and "spiritual."

What is this "ego-based ministry" that is collapsing? It is a style of ministry where the minister himself becomes the center of attention, the "big person," the "communicator." Ego-based ministry puts the minister at the center of everything. It is minister-as-hero. *He* (or she) is the issue. He is the one they talk about whenever the church is mentioned. The minister becomes "bigger than life." He "fills up the room" when he enters it. His personality dominates the entire church. He has the answers. He is confident, knows where he is going. He is a "great leader." He expects absolute loyalty from his people. He often makes himself the hero of his own stories and illustrations. His people retell his self-inflating stories and his image gradually becomes even bigger than he really is. Soon he tries to live up to the image he has created, and if he can't, he simply pretends to be what the hero-worshipers think he is (and want him to be). People idolize him.

He is now a "personality." He is in demand. If he is a visiting speaker, he totes along bundles of his cassette tapes to sell. People buy them. They are hungry for heroes — he might as well supply that need. If he has written, he will huckster his books and manuals. His credibility is based on the fact that he has "done it." So he tells story after story illustrating how he has "done it." We listen and applaud. We want to be like this man who has the answers. We buy his tapes and books. We attend his seminars. In fact, he really does have most of the answers for just about every church or personal problem . . . he *does*!

So, if he really has the answers, why is the church so fed up with this style of ministry? Because, without ever telling us so, the church has switched its basis of credibility. In the 1980s the key to being a hero was to have "done it." The bottom line was your track record, your growth, your size, your income. Back then we believed that there was some sort of secret method to get church growth. We wanted in on that secret. These people had it. The whole thing was almost gnostic! We wanted to discover the secret method and put it into practice here to get the kind of growth that our hero had. It was almost like those infomercials where the guy tells you how you can make millions on real estate right there in your own little town. We wanted to believe it was true. And, right there are people who testify that it worked for them!

But the '80s taught us two things that brought about the collapse of ego-based ministry. (It took until the mid-90s for it to really dawn completely on us.) First we finally discovered: There is no secret method for church growth. The secret method we wanted to discover didn't exist. There are many ways to grow a church, and most of them are so intertwined with the personality of the pastor, the church, and the local culture that they do not transfer from one place to another. With no single secret to discover, we became less enraptured with those who supposedly had the secret. But the second discovery was the final nail in the coffin. We discovered that some of our most successful heroes were spiritual frauds. They were phonies. They HAD been successful and had "done it." But they were morally corrupt. We now know for sure what we suspected all along — "Outward success and inward character are only loosely related." Maybe they are totally unrelated.

So the church is tired of heroes. Now we want honest, humble preachers — men of integrity — not great "communicators" or "great people." Men and woman who can build a church, get people truly saved, and see growth, yes. But preachers who first and foremost are godly, not "big men." Laymen have changed their taste in pastors too. "Godliness" may now even become one of the interview questions, not just a ministerial candidate's "track record" (as if being interviewed for football coach at a major university).

And the people's tastes in outside speakers have changed too. They no longer know for sure if this guy is really a man of character. They have been burned too many times. (Two of the five most popular Wesleyan camp speakers have morally fallen in the last five years.) They aren't sure they can trust any hotshot speaker. So they accept less pizzazz, fewer self-inflating stories. More honest confession, less flamboyance. More humility, fewer cassettes and books.

So the church has switched the basis by which it judges success. "Personality ministry" or "ego-based" ministry is collapsing. A totally new criterion is being introduced quietly everywhere — in the evangelical church and in The Wesleyan Church. This new criterion will be the basis of our "success" in the future. It will determine the style of ministry in a local church, who we pick as our models and heroes, and who we want as our leaders and preachers. So, what is that new criterion? That is the subject of the next essay.

1. Will the church ever really give up stars and heroes? Should it?

2. What are the problems associated with our hero-worship and star-studded Christianity?

3. What are the advantages of having people who are bigger than life, people we look up to?

4. What cultural and religious factors may have contributed to the collapse of "ego-based" ministry . . . why is it that people are increasingly disgusted with big egos in the ministry?

5. Think about why God sometimes uses somebody with a big ego to do an important task. Is it because all the humble people don't think enough of themselves to even try? What Bible leaders with big egos would you cite to show that God does use such people? What stories illustrate the danger of a big ego or pride?

CHARACTER-BASED MINISTRY

Many of us have sensed that the church is between one thing and another. We are in a period of transition in value systems. Our culture had its stars — Madonna, Michael Jackson, and O.J. Simpson. We had our own stars too. In fact, the church became literally star struck in the '80s. We had our own big men and big personalities. Their personalities filled up a room or conference center when they entered or spoke. And we rewarded them with power, wealth and honor. They became the church's totems, representing our highest values.

But while they were great men, they were not always good men. We assumed that an inner character supported all this external success. We figured that God would not permit such success, so many converts, such growth, such size, such influence, unless these great men were also good. Now we know better.

For these and other reasons the church is in the process of adopting some new beliefs. We never called a conference. We never published a findings report or a declaration. But there is a new creed emerging nonetheless. We are learning from our experience in the '80s. Through all the pain, the church is increasingly coming to believe these three propositions: (1) External success and internal character are either unrelated or only loosely related. (2) It is possible to have great external success without inner character. (3) It is also possible to have a good inner character without great external success.

We now know that numerical and financial success are not the rewards for being godly. External success and inner character are not tied tightly together. You can have either, you can have both, or you can have neither. These are our new beliefs. And, new beliefs create a new culture. Ego-based ministry is quietly being dethroned in the church. Sure, there are still many who worship this king, but they are like those who touted the Holy Roman Empire long after it crumbled. Ego-based ministry is going fast.

So where to next? What will be our new criterion of success? We are in a transition from skill-based ministry to character-based ministry. Character-based ministry. Character-based ministry is the future. The laity have been burned too. They increasingly want a pastor who is first of all a godly man, not just one who can do the job. Character-based ministry is about inner integrity, not just external success. It focuses on *being* more than *doing*. The heart before the hand, godliness before goals, spiritual vitality before vision. It is about being a person of integrity, whatever the cost. Our heroes of the future will be people who are close to God, stand for truth, do what is right, and pay the price.

If this notion is correct, we are in for a major shift in our criterion of success. There are massive implications for us in how we select people, praise them, reward them, collect their statistics, and anoint them as leaders. It is too early in the transition to consider all of the implications here, but there are two for us to consider right off the bat: (1) Longer pastoral terms. The laity can be star struck with a fellow's skills or ego in a month or week, but developing a character-based credibility will take years. (2) Suffering. After all, isn't that the best way for people to see your true character? These two implications are just a start. There are more, aren't there?

1. What is "character"? How do you know a person has it?

2. Jesus Christ was a man of character. How do you know this? What proves this to you? How does this apply to pastoral or lay leadership in the church?

3. List some people of obvious character — people worthy of being a hero even though they are not "big egos" or famous or (in spite of their fame), people who are clearly people of character and worthy of being looked up to.

4. What has happened in the secular culture in the last few decades which makes all "big-ego" heroes suspect?

5. Who in your own church do you look up to as paragons of character?

6. What tests character? When does it show?

IF IT'S NEW, I'M AGAINST IT

Most of the people who read my essays know that I am actively involved in Internet publishing and writing. I believe it will have a massive impact on study, research, communication, entertainment, and the church. However I have often faced others, some of them substantial denominational leaders, who dismiss the whole thing as a fad and irrelevant to the future. As a tribute to these doubting-Thomas leaders, I list the following sketch of the family tree of such leaders:

1455 Johannes Gutenberg invents the printing press, potentially increasing to lightning speed the slow process of hand-copying books, including the Bible. Friar Thomas grumbles, "Phooey, that impersonal pile of machinery will never replace the personal touch of our hand-copied Bibles."

1845 Samuel Morse's telegraph connects Baltimore and Washington, enabling messages to be transmitted almost instantly between the two cities. Reverend Thomas says, "Why in the world would anyone in Washington want to say something instantly to people in Baltimore? A letter will get there in several days."

1867 After winter ice jammed the East River, halting all water routes into and out of Manhattan, a variety of leaders propose connecting Manhattan to the other boroughs with bridges over and tunnels under the East River. Reverend Thomas says, "I doubt you could ever build a bridge over that river, and certainly never a tunnel under it — why it would leak!"

1877 Thomas Edison shows off his new machine, a phonograph. It talks or makes music when the crank is turned. Upon hearing it, Reverend Thomas remarks, "Well, there certainly would never be a use for something like a box of music for speaking to people in the church."

1879 News of Edison's patents for the electric light circulate. Reverend Thomas laughs heartily when someone suggests electrifying the church and starting an evening service. "Now why in the world would a church need electric lights? Oil lamps were good enough for Eutychus and St. Paul, they should be good enough for us. Besides when it gets dark, God intended humans to go to bed. This will have no effect on the church."

1899 Marconi demonstrates his wireless telegraph by sending a message across the English Channel through the air. Upon reading it in the newspaper, Reverend Thomas grouses, "What would England and France have to say to each other? And for certain, the church would never need to use such a communication device."

1903 Two Indiana bicycle shop owners, Wilbur and Orville Wright, successfully complete a three-mile flight in a new machine which flies in the air. Reverend Thomas lays down his newspaper and comments to his wife, "Why in the world would anyone want to fly? I doubt this will come to anything. Certainly it will have no impact on the church."

1913 Henry Ford introduces mass production, enabling several families in Reverend Thomas' church to purchase Model Ts. Rev. Thomas is dubious. "I'll stick with walking to my parishioners and use my trusty horse for the outlying folk. After all, it was good enough for John Wesley."

1922 As wires are strung, the telephone (invented by Alexander Graham Bell in 1876), is finally introduced into many houses in Reverend Thomas' town. He passes on installing a telephone with a chuckle. "How in the world would a minister use a telephone? You've got to go see people face to face."

1950 A. B. Dick's mimeograph invention (1887) is being widely adopted during the post-war period by many churches. In 1950 Rev. Thomas' pastor friend buys one with his own money. "What in the world would you do with that?" Rev. Thomas asks. Upon discovering that the pastor intends to print up his own worship bulletins, he is incredulous. "Why in the world would a local church print up its own bulletins? Can't the people hear the announcements?"

1961 A younger treasurer of the church asks the board for permission to secure one of the new electric adding machines to replace the old hand-cranked adding machine (based on the machine invented by Blaise Pascal in the 17th century). Rev. Thomas doubts the need for such a newfangled toy and asks, "What in the world is wrong with a simple, manual adding machine that churches have used for years . . . remember many of the smaller churches still use pencil and paper."

1976 A new hand-held electronic calculator emerges. It is touted to instantly solve difficult calculations for college students and could make the slide rule obsolete. Pastor Thomas sees the advertisement on TV and remarks, "That will never catch on — too expensive and not any better than our trusty electric adding machine over at the church."

1979 One of Pastor Thomas' fellow ministers purchases an Apple computer and uses it to run off labels for his midweek mailings. Magazines predict that every home will eventually have one or more personal computers. Thomas says, "Why in the world would a home need a computer? We don't even need one at the church. They're just a toy."

1980 Scientists predict that an entire library of information will eventually be written and stored on a single disk created with lasers. Glancing around his office walls, which display nearly a thousand books, Pastor Thom says, "They'll never have minister's resources on such disks — I doubt anything will come of it."

1981 The Xerox process invented by Chester Carlson in 1938 finally produces small photocopy machines at affordable prices. Even small offices can now purchase them. When a neighboring pastor talks of his church's new Xerox machine, Pastor Thomas remarks, "But they're too expensive for us . . . I'll stick with that old mimeograph machine I inherited."

1995 E-mail and the World Wide Web explode from the quiet innovator phase to the "early adopter" level with multiplied ministers going on line one after another. At a recent pastors' meeting Pastor Thomas was overheard saying, "Why in the world would a minister ever need to be on the Internet? This will have no effect on the church. I doubt anything will come of it."

2000 Pastor Thomas has adopted every single innovation invented since 1455, but now doubts anything will come of the newest and most recent inventions.

1. Some things *were* fads and "nothing came of them" in the last several decades. About which of these things was "Doubting Thomas" right? Are there others?

2. How do you think the Internet will affect how the church does its ministry and business?

3. The writer of these essays exhibits a curious blend of preserving the past yet moving into the future. He is hard to pin down as a conservative or a progressive. Does this reflect you too? On what things are you a "conservative" — you want to keep good things from the past? And on what things would you be "progressive" — desiring to utilize the newest and best innovations to move forward into the future?

4. Are things in the world getting "worse and worse" or are they gradually improving?

5. How do you connect the Bible's teaching about the "days of Noah" (which seems to indicate things will deteriorate), with the opposite notion of the mustard seed and other parables (which seems to suggest a more optimistic outlook)?

6. John Wesley (or sometimes his mother, Susanna) is quoted regarding innovations, trends, and styles as saying, "Do not be the first to adopt. Do not be the last." What is the idea behind this approach to the new?

TEN PERSUASIVE ARGUMENTS FOR STEALING CANDY BARS

1. Everybody does it.

I even know some Christians who steal candy bars.

2. You probably won't get caught.

Because the practice is so widespread, and there is so little enforcement, the chance of being caught is slim.

3. Even if caught, prosecution is doubtful.

You probably wouldn't be taken to court or tried anyway.

4. It doesn't involve much money.

Stealing a car, or a boat, or something like that — well, that's different. But candy bars cost so little; taking them is certainly not serious.

5. The owners will never miss it.

There are millions of candy bars circulating around our world. Who's going to miss one or two?

6. It will save you money.

Stealing candy bars on a regular basis can add up to a substantial savings. After all, we are to be good stewards of our money — and that means cutting expenses everywhere we can.

7. It will save you time.

Stealing candy bars saves time in the checkout line. Better yet, if you can steal them at work it will save a trip to the local candy store, or worse, a long wait for a mail-order supplier to send your bars.

8. The law is confusing.

I'm not a lawyer and you know how confusing legal matters are. Some say it is OK, others say don't. Hey, go ahead and take a few until they straighten out this mess and make it clear to all of us.

9. The owners are Christians anyway.

If the owners are Christians, we Christians should have a right to steal a few candy bars. After all, they shouldn't be trying to make money off other Christians.

10. It's for a good cause.

Now I might be persuaded that stealing for personal benefit is questionable, but certainly stealing for the congregation, choir, or Sunday school class wouldn't be wrong, would it?

Now, for ten persuasive arguments for photocopying copyrighted books, songs, and sheet music, or copying tapes, just read the list again.

1. This essay is satirical, but it makes a serious point. Sometimes church people justify stealing, especially if it is for a good cause. Why is stealing for the church easier than stealing for ourselves?

2. Is it really "stealing" to buy one sheet of choir music and copy it for the whole choir? Why or why not?

3. Is it "stealing" to make 20 copies of choir music, just to get things on one side of a sheet, if you have already bought 20 copies?

4. Is it stealing to borrow CDs or tapes from a friend and copy them off for personal use? Is it stealing to make copies of your own CDs or tapes?

5. Is it wrong to sell copies of sermons recorded at campmeetings without the permission of the speaker? Do you think preaching and singing are God's property and thus shouldn't be protected by copyright laws? Likewise, how do you feel about others using the local church's property for free?

6. How does the system work where churches pay a fee to copy songs to put on slides or an overhead screen?

TONGUES... ○ ○ ○
IS THERE A MIDDLE GROUND?

Few recent issues have produced so much conflict, dissension and division in the church of late. It's hard to stay in the middle of the road on this one. In most churches and denominations you are either "for 'em or against 'em." Division does that sort of thing — pushes people further over one edge or the other. And there is often only a narrow strip, right smack in the middle of the road — and that's where you'll likely get shot at from both sides (which is what this essay will bring). But, I ask, can we find a middle ground on this issue?

What are the two sides? In the ditch, off one side of the road are those infected with a good case of "Charis-mania." They speak in tongues every chance they get and insist that everyone else join them. Off in the other ditch are the "Charis-phobics," who are absolutely terrorized by any sign of tongues-speaking and are committed to stamping it out and driving Charismatics into the sea. [OK, I know there is a difference between Pentecostal, charismatic, and tongues-speakers ... don't write me on that, but that's beyond my purpose here.] Consider both ditches alongside the road:

"CHARIS-MANIA"

Off to one side, are those infected with extreme Charis-mania . . . they've fallen in love with speaking in tongues and believe it to be the master experience of religious life. These individuals might even insist that speaking in tongues is the great secret to powerful and victorious living. Or, that tongues-speaking is the only possible sign that a Christian is really Spirit-filled. To them, you either speak in tongues like they do, or you're not filled with the Spirit, period.

Those overtaken by Charis-mania cite scriptural cases in the book of Acts where tongues-speaking and Spirit-filling are associated: at Pentecost, at Cornelius' house in Caesarea, in Ephesus, and perhaps even implied in Samaria when Peter and John visited Philip. Where Charis-mania prevails, you'll hear arguments that you can't be filled with the Spirit unless you have this one, single, master evidence — speaking in tongues. But the real radicals are found among those who assert that you are not even saved unless you speak in tongues. Yikes!

The Charis-mania extreme refuses to quietly enjoy their own religious experiences in private. They want everyone else to have exactly the same ecstatic experiences they've had. They become "evangelistic" about persuading others to speak in tongues. And this is where the trouble starts. Once any individual's religious experience becomes the standard for others, dissension, strife and division are not far off.

The route to division and strife in a church often follows a familiar pattern: First, I claim some sort of personal, religious experience unique and powerful and special. Soon, I want others to have the same thing, so I testify privately about how wonderful this experience has been for me — what a difference it has made in my life! Soon I find myself "recruiting" others to get what I have.

If they do get it, two or three of us might start meeting together, perhaps in a Bible study. After all, we increasingly have much more in common with each other than with the rest of the church. Our group is so stimulating we begin inviting others to join us. Some do. Others get suspicious. We soon develop a burden for "the rest of the church" — which seems so shallow and lacking in power — even the pastor. We begin praying for the pastor (and the rest of the church) that they too will "get the power" like we have. Based on our newfound spiritual pizzazz, we just can't understand why the pastor seems so bland. "If he could just get a good case of what we have, then this church would really take off."

Gradually an attitude of spiritual superiority infects our group. Increasingly, we consider ourselves to be the "true church." Some people try to correct this, but we interpret their attempt as "persecution," assuming they want to stamp out the Holy Spirit's work. We begin grieving at the "spiritually dead leadership" of the church. We finally feel sadly compelled to leave, go somewhere else, or start our own church.

Isn't this how it happens sometimes? Ask me, I know. I come from the "holiness movement" which spread like wildfire about a hundred years ago, and pulled people out of Methodist churches in the same way — not over tongues, but over "entire sanctification." What starts out as a personal religious experience can wind up splitting a congregation in the end. People are hurt. Some get bitter. Nobody feels good about the whole affair, including God.

Anywhere this sort of thing has happened, and there are plenty of churches who have experienced it, an increasing number of folk rush over to the other extreme:

"CHARIS-PHOBIA"

These folk wind up off the other side of the road — they are terrified of anything related to the charismatic movement in any way. They especially fear "borderline charismatics," as they call them. This group not only opposes speaking in tongues, but wants no part of any worship style with "charismatic tendencies." They say, "If you give 'em an inch, they'll take a mile."

Charis-phobics enjoy pointing out prideful attitudes among charismatics, especially those who left their church. They even seem to rejoice when a popular charismatic leader falls into sin — pointing out that tongues-speaking apparently didn't help him live a holy life after all.

Charis-phobics want to keep a neat churchful of people just like themselves. Sometimes they feel compelled to assign themselves to "search-and-destroy" missions around the church, in order to discover and eliminate any charismatic "leaven." They sometimes tell these folk, "You'll simply feel more comfortable in another church — certainly *we* will feel more comfortable if you leave."

Charis-phobics see singing with raised hands, verbal shouts like "Amen" or "Hallelujah," worship choruses, clapping in services, or elongated standing-up-praise-times as signs "we're going charismatic." Figuring that the best way to avoid charismatic extremes is to steer as far as possible to the other side of the road, they resist the introduction of anything which even originated in the charismatic movement.

This group fears charismatics so much they remind others that tongues could be "of the Devil." They cite Bible illustrations like Pharaoh's magicians who were able to perform miracles using Satan's power. They are quick to sense a charismatic conspiracy underfoot, and are the first to suggest "we need to get control of this before it spreads." They enjoy telling others that tongues-speaking is common in some cults and non-Christian religions, satisfyingly assuming they have proven its satanic origins.

As soon as someone with "charismatic leanings" starts attending church, the Charis-phobic lookouts begin raising the alarm, "Watch out, sooner or later they'll split this church." Charis-phobics delight in setting up scientific tests for charismatics like, "If you've really got the gift, then record your tongues-speaking, and we'll take it to three different people with the gift of interpretation and see if their interpretation is identical." They gleefully point out that there is no record that Jesus spoke in tongues, and the one New Testament church where it prevailed was the most sin-plagued, carnal, divided church of the New Testament. Charis-phobics forget that the enemy is the Enemy, not the charismatics.

MIDDLE GROUND?

So, could there be a middle ground in all this? Is there a place we could meet which avoids the radical extremes of "Charis-mania," yet stops short of running off the "Charis-phobic" side of the road too? I suspect there is. And I don't occupy the middle ground on this. But I'm willing to talk about it. How about this as a discussion starter:

1. There was tongues-speaking in Bible times.

To deny it is to be unfaithful to the Bible. Tongues were not limited to Pentecost either, but occurred at other times as well. Granted, there are different kinds of tongues. The event at Pentecost seems to be a miracle of unlearned languages. In Corinth the tongues was a kind of "glossolalia" or unknown language. What occurred in Acts beyond Pentecost could have been either or both. But it would be dishonest to clip out the tongues sections of God's Word and toss them in the wastebasket because "we've already made up our minds on this." It's right there — as plain as the words in the Word.

2. Tongues seemed to be primarily a "sign."

They seem to be a miraculous incident designed to convince unbelievers, at least Paul told the Corinthians so. This experience was not to be some sort of spiritual Mountain Dew, designed to tickle one's spiritual innards. The post-Pentecost tongues-speaking in Acts was primarily an "echo effect" of Pentecost, used by God to affirm that the Holy Spirit was being poured out on a population far broader than just the Jerusalem Jews. The primary purpose seems to be a miracle sign to unbelievers, or to confirm that God accepted non-Jews too . . . it was not for personal stimulation and delight.

3. The Pentecost tongues communicated the gospel.

Each person heard the gospel in his own language. The miracle itself proved little — in fact, the crowd simply presumed the speakers were drunk. It was the gospel message which got through, in each person's own language, which brought 3,000 souls into the Kingdom that day. Perhaps there should be more seeking of this kind of tongues today, or at least "whatever it takes" to see three thousand conversions in a single service?

4. Public tongues-speaking in Corinth was a problem.

If other New Testament churches used tongues in their services, I don't know about it. I do know about Corinth. In this church public tongues-speaking was a problem, and contributed to spiritual pride, disorder and division. Paul, more concerned about the gospel than subsidiary issues (he wouldn't even argue over baptism!), seems to permit the practice to continue in Corinth, though he severely limits it. He did not promote it, or even mention the issue to any other churches that I can find.

5. A church or denomination is free to worship how it wants to.

We are not free to change the gospel, but churches, even entire denominations, are free to determine what they will and won't do in public services. If a church decides they'll primarily use choruses in worship, fine. If another sticks with hymns, that's fine too. If a church wants to have services where they sing an hour, run the aisles, toss their hats in the air, "get blessed" or warble like birds, have at it. If another church chooses not to do these things, that's fine too. In my mind, all any church is "required" to do is practice the sacraments and preach the gospel. Beyond that, they've got a right to design their own worship practices, including or excluding this or that based on their own cultural, theological, and traditional preferences.

6. If someone privately prays in tongues, so what?

Who will dictate what someone says or does in their private prayer closet? Will you? Not me. Even the Pope won't do that. Pray any way you want, as far as I am concerned. The trouble here is not what you do in your private prayer closet, but what you say when you come out. Remember Jesus' rules for private prayer? He taught us to pray in secret, then make sure nobody knew about it. To Jesus, private prayer is so personal and intimate that we are to keep it to ourselves — so much so that we are to be a bit deceptive, to pretend we aren't doing it at all! If someone prays with agonizing groans, in a falsetto voice, sings their prayers, lies prostrate in the cellar, or prays with a language I don't recognize, what is that to me if they keep it to themselves when they come out? What am I going to do, send inspectors to their prayer closet? To me, the problem isn't how a person prays in private — but how they might broadcast it later that causes trouble. Does this make sense?

7. The gospel is the middle ground.

Christians have a tremendous capacity to get off track and preoccupied with less than primary things. Paul recognized this and warned us repeatedly that the central issue is to "preach Christ and Him crucified." When anything else pushes its way into the center, the Cross of Christ gets shoved out of the way. The Cross is the central issue, not choruses, clapping, hand-raising, or how a person prays in private. When anything is elevated above the Cross, we can be dangerously close to idolatry.

I am not a charismatic. But it seems to me that there's got to be a "middle ground" somewhere on this matter, at least for us non-charismatic churches. Shouldn't more of us try to find it? That's what I think.

1. Is there a middle ground on this issue or can't one church contain folk of both types?

2. If you were to draw a continuum on this issue, where would you place your own church? Where would you place yourself?

3. How would you connect tongues-speaking with other emotional manifestations like shaking, quaking, running the aisles, shouting, being slain in the Spirit, and "getting blessed"?

4. Does a local church have the right to limit what people want to do in its public service, or can any individual speak, sing, or dance based on his or her own declaration that "God told me to do this"?

5. How far do you think a local church should go in restricting what its members do in their private, personal prayer life?

6. Do you know of any examples where churches have forged a "middle ground" — where people from a charismatic background and a non-charismatic background live in peace?

7. What Bible passages speak of unity and peace in the church, and what price should we be willing to pay for those qualities?

THE "GENERATION SKIP"

In the last decade or so many older people were astonished when younger pastors dressed up in sweaters and did away with all the hymnals in favor of an overhead screen. Out went robed choirs and the organ, and in came praise teams and drums. Out went the pulpit, in came a "stage" atmosphere. Drama was introduced along with a fast-paced, MTV-like production. Older people were horrified. They started complaining that the "church is becoming worldly." Younger people, however, insisted that organs, hymnals, and formal dressing for worship were generational innovations and not inspired methods.

What's going on here? Why is there such conflict and divergent opinion regarding worship styles today? There are many factors, but certainly one of the reasons is the "generation skip." Traditionally the church has had an orderly transfer of power and leadership from sixty-year-old people to adults in their fifties. As the retired older people passed out of the picture (even though they stayed on the board, they became less influential), the functional leadership in a church would pass to leaders in their fifties. These "younger-older" people had some different views than their elders, but generally speaking, change was incremental and orderly. As change was introduced, those in their sixties accepted the adjustments as necessary adaptations to the newer fifty-year-old leaders. We had orderly change and transfer of power without great revolution.

But this is not occurring in the church today. The baton of power has skipped the fifty-something generation and is being passed all the way down to the forties-thirties generation. Why?

First, there are few of the fifties generation around. Some church leaders call this the "lost generation." This crowd was born in the late 1930s and early 1940s. It is the most under-represented decade in the church population today. So, there are simply not many fifty-something leaders around to take up the power.

But there is a second factor as well. This generation has produced few strong leaders. Leith Anderson calls this generation "men who implement other men's dreams." While there are some impressive exceptions, by and large there are not a lot of strong, aggressive leaders emerging out of the fifties generation. America saw this in the last presidential election. The leadership passed from a man in his sixties to a man in his forties . . . the fifties generation was simply skipped.

And that brings us to the "generation skip" in the church. Right on the heels of the fifties "lost generation" or "silent generation" is a huge "Baby Boom" generation, now in their forties and thirties. Unlike their fifty-something elder brothers and sisters, this crowd is aggressive, opinionated, insistent, demanding and often arrogant. They will not be silent. They will not wait until they are older to take charge.

All of this produces an unusual situation in a local church. Leadership often has transferred from the sixties crowd to those in their fifties (with a sprinkling of younger people who often followed along until they were in their fifties). More recently, leadership has skipped the fifties generation and passed down to the forties-thirties generation. When this crowd gets control it makes changes — and the sooner the better, in their opinion.

This shows up most clearly in worship styles. The forties-thirties crowd is casual, quality-oriented, fast-paced, and exceptionally absorbed with positive things. For them "classic rock music" *is* traditional music — it is the only secular music style they have ever known. Since they have also been raised on television, they like drama. They like to do things as a team. Instead of having an individual "song leader," they insist on having leadership shared between men and women. They like organization, management, leadership, Xerox machines, computers, FAX machines, and cellular telephones. They want the church to run as well as their businesses. All of this has caused conflict and division in many churches. To the pastors and younger leaders who have adopted a forties-thirties worship style, older people say, "We want our church back." Other churches have developed two separate services — one for the older generation and the other for the younger crowd. This too causes conflict. Older people suspect they are simply being asked to "show up and pay your tithe" so that the younger pastor and Baby Boomer board can do what they really love — "entertain the Baby Boomers in the other service."

So what's a church to do? The older generation must recognize that the extraordinary amount of change they are experiencing is a result of leadership passing down two generations at once. Older folk must adapt to "twenty years of change in five years." While it is hard to do, the "generation skip" necessitates this adaptation. Boycotting services, withholding tithes, and carrying on a destructive, critical telephone campaign is not the answer. Neither is clamping down so severely that the younger folk are chased out to the thousands of new "Boomer churches." Accepting the fact that we're having two generations of change crammed into a single generation helps older folk understand why "they've taken our church away from us."

But we younger leaders have to be more careful too. We must be far more sensitive to the needs of the older crowd. Face it, we Baby Boomers are the most self-centered generation our country has ever known. We talk about being "need-oriented" or "targeting the audience," but what we often really mean is "meeting the needs of people like us" and targeting our own interests. We say we are being "seeker sensitive," but in fact we are often merely designing the service to fit our own likes and style of music. We then totally forget our need-meeting principles when it comes to anyone over fifty years of age! We devour dozens of books describing the needs and culture and value systems of Baby Boomers and Baby Busters and those in "generation thirteen." But we seldom read anything — even if it were available — about the needs of people in their fifties and sixties, or older. Let's confess it — we are far more interested in meeting the needs of our generation than in meeting the needs of the older generation. Those of us who are leaders in the forties-thirties generation must be far more sensitive to ministering to all generations, not just "people like us."

And finally, all of us must learn to compromise, to give some and take some, to win some and lose some. Come on, be honest, it won't hurt people in their sixties and fifties to learn a few new praise choruses, even if you think they are shallow, lacking in theology, and repetitive. And come on, Baby Boomers, it really won't hurt your spiritual life to sing some of those grand old songs out of a hymnal. All of us must be a bit more pliable, more "easily entreated," and more understanding of other generations in the church. If the generations cannot get along in the church, it will ultimately lead to "generational congregations." Baby Boomers will simply plant their own churches and forget the older generation, allowing those churches to decline into obscurity.

Too much is at stake to fight over these issues. Balance is the objective. And we will only achieve balance as the older generation accepts change and the younger generation now in power introduces change incrementally and with sensitivity, inspired by self-less love. With a bit of understanding and a giant portion of God's grace, we can work this out.

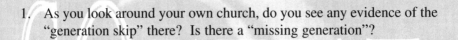

1. As you look around your own church, do you see any evidence of the "generation skip" there? Is there a "missing generation"?

2. Why is it that churches sometimes lose an entire generation? What could happen to make us lose people in their 20s today in our church?

3. How do you predict the "Boomers" will react to becoming the older generation . . . how will they handle an orderly transfer of leadership to the generations under them?

4. The writer here calls for a little elasticity on the worship issue. Where do you think you might be a little rigid yourself and could use a bit of softening?

5. Try listing all the changes in worship which a 70-year-old church member might have experienced. Now, if change occurs in the next 50 years at the same rate, what would church be like for you?

FIFTEEN REASONS TO UNPLUG YOUR TV ONCE IN A WHILE

1. TV is the number one secularizing influence in most Christians' lives.

The Devil has a million ways to get at you, but television is his best way of "getting into your head." TV is the most effective influence to make you a less committed Christian. If you keep watching it, you'll become even more secular in your mind-set.

2. TV is most Christians' biggest time robber.

We all waste time on other things, but TV is the biggest black hole of all for most Christians. What does TV time take you away from? It is time which could be spent on better things. Working in your wood shop. Working in the garden. Spending time with your kids. Having a chat with your wife. Going for a walk. In fact, the average person logs more time in front of the TV than in doing anything else, except sleeping. The average American adult spends three hours per day watching TV. That's 52 complete 24-hour days every year. We adults spend a full 12 years of our life span watching TV. (We spend four months in Sunday school.)

I sometimes complain, "I don't have enough time." But the truth is, I have the same amount of time Jesus Christ had — 24 hours each day. It's not how much time we "have," but how we use this time that is our problem. I watch far less TV than the average adult, but it's still my single biggest time robber. What about you?

3. TV softens us toward sin.

The television is highly effective at brainwashing. It seduces us into accepting sins the Bible clearly rejects. Its storytelling and interview formats raise feelings of sympathy, compassion and understanding for behaviors I know are wrong. TV has already made me softer on divorce. Right now it is trying to convince me that marital unfaithfulness is normal — even attractive. And increasingly, TV will persuade you and me that homosexual behavior is simply the alternative lifestyle of people "born this way."

If you and I keep watching TV on a regular basis, it will surely convince us to soften, then fully accept, these sins. Have you watched how this happens to you? We are first outraged by what we see. We angrily switch to another channel or turn it off completely. But, over time, the outrage dissipates. Eventually we allow the offense to pass by with only a verbal rejection like, "That's not true," or "That doesn't fit with what the Bible says." Finally, we quit making verbal comments and hardly notice. Sin has lost its shock. The more we watch TV, the more "understanding" we'll become toward sin. We really ought to unplug our TV, shouldn't we? At least for a week once in a while, just to show it who's boss.

4. TV presents a false view of marriage.

Because it is an emotional medium, TV constantly focuses on falling in love, having sex, and breaking up. This is a false view of marriage. Most of marriage is, well . . . boring. It's not all stimulation and excitement, with wild and wonderful trips to Acapulco. Marriage is mostly routine, based on commitment — not the romantic ideal presented on TV.

And beyond this false view of marriage, TV is constantly biased against the biblical pattern of marriage. While two-thirds of U.S. adults are married, television constantly focuses on singleness and single-parenting, and brainwashes us to believe married life is neither average nor normal. And even when it does feature married couples, these couples are awful examples of a regular marriage, let alone a Christian marriage. Marriage is tough enough work in today's world, without the influence of television dragging us away from the biblical model.

5. TV gives me a distorted view of religion.

Secular shows are constantly portraying ministers as corrupt, greedy, greasy hypocrites. I don't like that. I don't want your kids being brainwashed against preachers and the ministry. But while preachers do poorly, religion itself does little better. The media's anti-religion bias is deep. Researchers from Duke, Northwestern, and the University of

Dayton studied 100 episodes of prime-time TV shows, including 1,464 speaking characters and 70 hours of programming. Ninety-five percent of the people showed no discernible religious affiliation whatsoever. And of the 5% which made some reference to religion (mostly to prayer, such as "thank God" or something similar), a full half of these presented the religious message in a negative light. This shouldn't surprise me. Only 7% of TV executives attend church regularly, while 97% are pro-abortion and 80% pro-homosexual. It shouldn't shock us that television constantly brainwashes us toward a negative and distorted view of religion. I suppose we might argue that our minds are already made up. But what does this do to children? And religious programming is no better. Religious TV portrays such a sick view of true religion that viewing secular programming might be safer.

6. TV affects your vocabulary.

I haven't started saying all the things I've heard on television, but I'm far less shocked now when I hear them. Are you? And I wonder, how long will it be until we start saying the words we hear? For instance in the last decade, have you noticed a significant increase in the use of God's name in a casual way by Christians? Is this somehow connected with the frequent use of God's name on TV? Do you remember when you first heard this, how you reacted? It was probably clear to you that this was a violation of God's third commandment. In fact, using God's name in a casual way is the clearest violation of that commandment you can imagine. Now the casual use of God's name is finding its way into the language of Christians. How long will it be before you allow yourself to say "My Lord," or "Oh my God," or "For God's sake"?

But it's not just God's name. Television constantly tries to adjust all of your vocabulary. You can hear it every day. TV is constantly correcting, constantly teaching, constantly "discipling" us. It tries to teach us to say "partner" instead of "wife." It wants you to say "in a relationship" instead of "married," and "gay" instead of "homosexual." It is so effective at teaching us what is right and wrong in speech, that gradually the vocabulary of the world seems much more appropriate than that of the Bible. But, along with this new vocabulary come the world's values. I don't like what the TV does to our vocabulary. And what this new vocabulary does to our values. Do you?

7. TV constantly models put-down humor.

It's most evident in shows like *The Simpsons*, *Rosanne*, and *Married . . . With Children*. But it's everywhere else as well. The relational modeling of TV is to deride others and criticize and put down loved ones. All this is done for the sake of humor. And it works. It is humorous. No wonder these same kinds of critical put-downs show up at home, in schools and at church. TV is a bad model for interpersonal relationships. It makes it easier for us to use put-down humor. Do you think so?

8. TV promotes the sin of materialism.

Why would advertisers spend millions of dollars if their advertisements did not cause me to want things? TV engenders coveting, materialism and idolatry — finding joy in things. How much has this "materialistic pornography" influenced me already? What has it already persuaded me to find happiness in . . . besides God? What has the TV taught me to want? To want so badly that I consider it a need? I should simply unplug it, shouldn't I?

9. TV is a social evil.

It's like alcohol, or tobacco, or gambling. The net result is socially negative. TV executives argue that there is no connection whatsoever between violence on television and crime in the streets, or between TV's sexual titillation and the behavior of the individuals watching these programs. Yet, the same TV executives will collect a million dollars for a 30-second advertisement during the Super Bowl. How do they collect money for these advertisements? Who pays for them? Why would advertisers pay such sums if the medium has no effect whatsoever on behavior? C'mon. Quit kidding us! TV *does* change the way we act. The average child sees 8000 killings on TV by the eighth grade. Is this in no way connected to the fact that violent crime is up 560% over the last 30 years? So, even if the TV had absolutely no effect on me personally, we ought to unplug it — simply as a social protest or boycott against the evil it promotes in society.

10. TV depresses educational achievement.

The studies are decisive. The more TV children watch, the less studying they do, the later they will stay up at night, and the more tired they will be the next day at school. The more TV students watch, the lower they score on achievement tests. Besides these proven facts, TV works against reading and discussion, two primary ways people learn. But what if I'm an empty-nester and all the kids are gone? What does it do to my educational achievement? Does it inspire me to read more? Discuss things more? Does it define the really deep issues? What issues does television raise which will be around in 100 years? Even ten years? I'm afraid TV depresses even your own learning, not just your children's learning. Does your TV watching have the net effect of increasing your learning?

11. TV is the great "agenda setter."

It irritates me. It embarrasses me too. Part of the reason I watch TV is to "keep up." To make sure I am "current," up-to-date, and "in the know." Television tells me what is important to talk about at coffee break, over lunch, with fellow travelers at the airport. The great sin in modern society is to be "out of touch." I want to be aware of your world, so I can talk intelligently about what is going on.

The trouble is, what the TV tells us is important really isn't. It is trivial, silly, even idiotic. A half dozen years ago or so it constantly instructed us to talk about Michael Jackson, the Bobbits, and Tonya Harding. Remember them now? Or how long will we really remember the "story of the century" — the O.J. Simpson trial? Every year TV will have a whole new agenda. Not one of these things is really important at all, let alone biblically important. TV-watching causes us to adopt a secular agenda in our discussions. We all need to talk more about God, godliness, holiness, righteousness and the eternal truths, not the passing trivia of the TV agenda. Do you ever resent being controlled by this one-eyed master in your family room?

12. Even the news doesn't redeem TV.

I wish it did, because I'm one of those persons with a special affinity for CNN and C-SPAN. But to be honest, most of the news is not about the eternal issues facing men and women today. Since local news shows generate significant income for local TV stations, they fall prey to the tremendous pressure to grab ratings by scandalous stories, titillating topics, and staged video. Murders, rapes, tragedy, and a host of stories reflecting a dangerous world are the constant fare. The more I watch, the more I'm taught that people are not to be trusted and the world is a dangerous place. National news is worse. I remember how I was glued to CNN during the Gulf War. It seemed like such an important thing at the time. But, now that I reflect on it, just what was I watching? I was watching the terror of war — thousands of people being killed, sent to eternity without God — and I watched in my living room, with a snack, watching it all as if it was an entertaining video game. Shame on me! Even the news hasn't redeemed the overall negative effect of television.

13. TV is addictive.

Sixty-four percent of Americans say TV has a negative effect on family life, according to Gallup. A full two-thirds say that TV has a negative effect on children, and 62% argue that TV promotes negative values. Then why do we watch? Because it is a habit. TV is the "plug-in drug." It is more addictive than tobacco or alcohol or pornography. How do you know you are addicted? You can't stop! Several years ago I tried

to persuade thousands of people to unplug their TVs for just one week — the first week of the year. It was a colossal flop. I might have had better success getting people to give up eating. Indeed even a food fast would go over better than a TV fast. Americans are addicted. They won't give it up. Even reading this essay won't do it. Reading this essay only serves to remind us of our addiction; it probably won't inspire many to actually unplug a TV — even for a week.

14. It's nearing time to vote.

I don't mean in a political election. I mean to vote for something bigger. Christians in North America are rapidly coming to the place where we are going to have to "vote" — either for the culture or against it. Many Christian leaders are increasingly convinced that the only Christians in the future will be those who have "come out" of the culture to live different lives — based on the values of the Bible, not the latest values of the most recent talk show. Perhaps we do not yet live in "Sodom." But once we do, separation is the only option. When this time comes (and it may not be far off), my hunch is that many Christians will vote to stay in Sodom. They will have been so seduced by the world that they will keep on trying to be "salt" until they eventually "lose all their savor." Yet a few — a "remnant" — will vote to reject the culture and will start to live their lives on Christian principles and behaviors. It has happened dozens of times throughout history. It may be about to happen again. When that time comes, how will you vote? Will you be so softened and seduced by Sodom that you'll try to stay in Sodom with an anemic attempt to "be a witness"? Or will you have the guts to reject Sodom's culture and become "peculiar" or "separate"? If you can't make a little decision on something like unplugging your television — even for one week — how will you be able to make a decision on the really big vote coming later? This could be a good test for us.

15. Because of where TV is going.

Anyone who has carefully studied the TV industry gets a feel for where it's headed. In the future, we will have 500 cable and satellite channels to watch, providing a vast array of "whatever you want." Since cable and satellite are not restrained by broadcast standards, TV will be able to provide even more of "what people want." What do they want? They want sex. They want violence. They want nudity. They want blood. No, they don't *say* they want these things. In fact, they condemn them noisily in all surveys, acting as if they're the silent "moral majority." They condemn them — but they still watch such shows. They consistently drive up the ratings of shows featuring sex and violence. Titillation sells. And TV is about selling. It is about ratings. When we only had three channels, the TV executives provided some restraint among themselves. But with 500 channels, the competition will drive all of the shows to feed the base desires of men and women. Will TV get worse? The answer is obvious.

And what about interactive television? In the future, we will no longer just watch a couple go to bed or undress, we will be able to control their actions interactively. In the future, we will see a merger of the TV, the CD-ROM, the computer and the phone line. From *watching* to *directing* actions of sex or violence is a leap of significant moral consequences.

And all this is just the beginning. In the next fifteen years, homosexual "love" will be normal. Total nudity will be common. The "seven deadly words" will be unleashed, and we will hear everything imaginable (and quite a bit we can't yet imagine). God will be openly mocked. There will be "artistic joking," picturing goats, women, or two lesbians hanging on a cross. There will be direct promotion of anti-Christ values and, just perhaps, even promotion of the Antichrist himself. Certainly, this is where it will go, won't it? All you have to do is continue the line on the graph — project the rate of past change into the future.

But all of this will happen gradually. That's the terror of television. It seduces us. It tempts us a tiny bit at a time, never overtly, and always with our willing participation — we go along. So most of us will gradually accommodate all of these things, and worse. Why not? Most of us now watch things we never dreamed we'd watch ten years ago. How did we get here? Gradually.

1. Is TV really as deadly as this writer suggests it is?

2. Do you think the television has as strong a hold on Christians as this writer suggests? Could most Christians make it through a TV-less week?

3. Most Evangelicals say, "I don't watch TV that much." But studies show that Evangelicals watch *more* TV than their secular counterparts. What do you think of these facts?

4. The writer of this essay assumes most Christians won't actually ever unplug their TVs, but will be gradually seduced into accepting things more and more contrary to the Bible. Do you agree or disagree with him? What evidence would you offer?

5. How can a family go TV-less without appearing to be legalistic or judgmental toward others? Do you know any families who have taken this route successfully?

6. What would it actually take to get you to totally unplug your TV and quit watching? What would you have to see or hear that would cross the line and be the "last straw" for you? Write it out on a slip of paper and collect them together as a group in your church. Re-read them in five years . . . maybe sooner.

7. Is there any cultural influence in biblical times parallel to the TV's influence today? What was the Bible's conclusion on dealing with it?

ARE YOU DOWNHEARTED?

The old song called it "downhearted." We call it *depressed* now, but it's the same thing. I recently spoke with a man who was wallowing in discouragement. He admitted that he simply sat around watching TV most of the time, feeling sorry for himself. He had been treated pretty roughly by some people over the last two years. And, even though the people who hurt him were now out of his life, he just couldn't get back into gear again. He said, "I feel like I'm trudging through deep muck — every step takes a big effort."

Ever feel this way? I have. What should you do when discouragement sets in? I asked several older men and two psychology professors what advice they'd give. Here is a summary of that advice for the downhearted:

1. Take action.

Do something. Start moving. Begin a new habit. Take a walk at the end of each day. Start playing racquetball, start jogging, start chopping wood, start anything . . . just begin some new regular habit. A person seldom escapes periods of lethargy instantaneously. Usually you climb out of the pit one rung at a time, often precipitated by starting one new habit at a time . . . not always spiritual ones.

2. Focus on others.

The most serious impact of discouragement is an inordinate preoccupation with your own situation. The worse you feel, the more you think about how badly you feel. Try to find some way to meaningfully get involved in the lives of others. This may seem especially preposterous advice for a person who is a minister, for instance, who does this for a living, but in times of discouragement even ministers can wind up ministering professionally but not personally. If you are a minister or lay person, find an opportunity to minister personally to one or several people — they will grow as a result of it. You'll likely discover your feelings of depression vanishing gradually.

3. Bury your past through forgiveness.

Depression and discouragement sometimes spring from the soil of injustice. You have been hurt unjustly. People have been unkind, un-Christlike, sinful, carnal, bitter, angry, or unfair to you. The route to release from this painful past lies through the grace of forgiveness. This is the greatest power you have. The only way to find release from this pain is to say, "I forgive them." You don't feel like it. But forgiveness is not a feeling . . . it is a choice. If you can make this choice, you may find new freedom and release, and maybe even a fresh burst of energy.

4. Set some achievable goals.

You're probably not going to leap out of this pit overnight. But by setting some simple goals, which you know you can achieve, you might bring back the sense of forward movement again. Maybe set a goal to take a one-mile walk once a week during this month. Or to read one book. Set some goals which you can start achieving, make a chart to check them off, and do it. Your success at accomplishing these things will breed more success.

5. Get accountability.

Your tendency will be to keep this discouragement to yourself. After all, Christians aren't supposed to be depressed. "Are you downhearted? NO NO NO!" the old song went. So we Christians cheerfully welcome people to the services when we feel only gloom inside. You probably feel like a hypocrite. You need someone to talk with. Find someone you know who will respect your confidentiality and make you accountable. You need a contact who will lovingly and gently — yet firmly — lead you out of the pits.

6. Get into the Word.

David in the Bible experienced similar times of discouragement and depression. There are a number of gloomy psalms which are ideal for this time in your life. Perhaps it is better to steer clear of the jubilant psalms, as if you can sing the blues away. Instead, read through all of Psalms and find the ones which especially reflect how you really feel. Then, keep going back to the same ones, reading them — even memorizing them —

and quoting them to the Lord. Just watch . . . this will reestablish communication with God so that the dryness resulting from discouragement will begin to disappear. At age 33 I experienced almost two years of ministerial discouragement. The psalms I came to own then were 77, 13, 28, and 42.

7. Hang in there.

This discouragement will be in your past some day. Take heart, it will! Perhaps it's trite, and of little help to you now, but it is true: this too will pass. It may take several months, it may take another year — but one of these days you'll be on top of things again. Most ministers walk through this "slough of despond" sooner or later. In fact, this seems to be one of the common threads running through all the great Christians' lives. Just keep slogging forward — the hill ahead has a wonderful view!

1. Have you ever experienced an elongated bout of depression? Not just an occasional "blue Monday" but a "blue every day"? How did you recover?

2. What role does chemical imbalance play in some of these problems? Should you even try to recover through spiritual means and self-help if the problem is really a chemical imbalance? What do you think?

3. How can you tell if another person is depressed? What are the signs?

4. What is the best way to minister to a depressed person? How is it different from helping a grieving person?

5. Who in the Bible had long bouts with depression . . . and how did they deal with it?

6. Perhaps more important, how can a person *prevent* depression? What tips would you offer to keep a person's head above the waters of depression?

A Personal Grief Journal

In the space of a few months, I lost both my father, Leonard Drury, and my brother, Elmer Drury. During the two years following their deaths, I kept a journal. Originally it was a private journal and was never intended to be shared with others. However, like all experiences of life, especially the difficult ones, we are being equipped to help others travel where we ourselves have passed. After sharing copies with one, then another, then many others going through the grieving process; after discovering that my words often spoke for them what they could not say for themselves, I decided to make it available publicly. If it has been several years since you lost a loved one, this journal may speak to you. If you have not yet experienced grief, or it happened long ago, this journal may enable you to help a friend in grief.

What follows are excerpts from my personal journal — one man's journey through the shadow of death.

At first I was simply numb. At the funeral I barely cried, wasn't emotional, and didn't exactly know how to act. No one taught me how to grieve. There are no classes in grief. I didn't know how to cry and get it over with. And I felt jealous about others who seemed to be able to cry openly, somehow releasing their grief with each heaving sob. Within weeks my only brother dies, followed by my Dad's death.

I busied myself with rearranging life in my mind to account for the loss. No longer could I call my Dad to tell him some bit of news I had picked up about which preacher was preaching a trial sermon where. No longer could I even hope for a few hours with my brother Elmer to talk about what a mess the church was in and how we seemed to know exactly how to fix it.

Actually, I didn't do these kinds of things very often, but I could have. That's what I miss so much, being able to talk, call, write, visit. Now I feel abandoned. I am all alone. Sure, there is Sharon, my Mom, JoAn . . . all precious women. But where are the men I loved so dearly? Dad, I need you . . . now more than ever. Elmer, where are you now? I've got a big decision ahead of me and I need to talk to you. Now. Silence. Deafening silence. They can't answer me now. They are beyond my reach. All my hungering for one more talk is in vain. They are gone. Forever. They will never come to me. I will go to them.

People don't help much when you're grieving. They try. Generally they fail. They don't know what to say. That's the problem; they think they have to say something. Mostly they'd do better just being there. But, for most people, they don't know how to handle a person in grief. We make them nervous. I can see their desperate looks when they encounter me. "Should I talk about it?" they say to themselves. I can see their nervousness as they try to decide what to say. Whatever they decide doesn't matter. I can't stand it when they talk. I can't stand it when they don't.

It's hard to figure out the effect of grief on the rest of life. I feel so lonely, so abandoned, forsaken, deserted. But most of all I feel lazy. I never realized how debilitating grief is. It's as if I am trudging through waist-deep snow. Every step is work. My life is running in slow motion. I feel tired, worn out, sleepy. Is this connected with grief? I've never been a lazy person. Motivated . . . whirlwind . . . aggressive, these are the words used to describe me. But right now I'm lazy. Motivation has leaked out.

"He's with God," they all tell me now. Or they say, "He's in God's hands." A few say, "Isn't it good to know he was ready?" They all say, "God knows best, doesn't He?" It is as if I am a first-grader. I guess these are the kinds of things you are supposed to say to grieving people. Like, "How are you doing today?" Or, "Looks like it's going to rain." Such is the hollow small talk which lubricates social life.

People say these things because they don't know what to really say. They think it helps. It doesn't.

Why did God let this happen? In a way I could have handled it better five years earlier or five years later. Why now? If God is God then can't He plan better than this? This is the year I most need my Dad. I know he wasn't much anymore . . . kidneys gone, heart barely beating, legs amputated . . . but his mind was still there. And his spirit. And that's what I need now. I need to talk to him. I want one more quiet little chat about where I'm headed. I want to hear one more time his quiet affirming confidence in his son's "doing a great work for God." I miss this.

I used to dread driving 12 hours to see him. The kids would get cranky, Sharon would be so worn out, and sleeping on the floor would sometimes take a week to recover from. I did it more than 20 times those last two years. And during those visits there was often less than five minutes of really meaningful conversation. Just five minutes. I'd drive to China for those five minutes now.

I wasn't really that close to my brother. At least the way some families are. We seldom wrote to each other. Only occasionally did we call each other. And the times we got together were usually limited to a few hours or so. He was on his way through town and would stop at my home or office for a few hours. Or, I would pass through his town and stop for an evening of visiting. Occasionally our travel schedules would cross on the road and we'd catch a lunch or a coffee break together. I suppose the total time we spent together in an average year would not exceed a few days.

Why do I miss him so? How could these few hours, with months between, be so important to me now? How could this loss make such a difference in the rest of the hours? I don't understand. I do know that all 365 days of my year are now quite different because of the loss of these few hours.

But, why? Why him? Why both? Why now? These are questions too big for me to answer. Only God knows. And He won't tell me.

Mom is here with us for her first winter alone. She's still in a daze. Barely remembers the dates. Then she hurt her back walking in the mall — a crushed vertebra. I cry foul! It's not fair, God. She cared for Dad

all those years . . . pouring herself out for him . . . never going to the doctor herself to get the care she really needed . . . imprisoned in the house as full-time nursemaid . . . now, for the first time in years she can go to the mall without worrying about Dad . . . and her vertebra crushes. It's just not fair. Please God, give her some good years of painless joy now. It's her turn, You know.

Grief is a strange thing . . . it's periodic. It goes away, seemingly forever, then returns with a renewed vengeance. Sometimes I think, "I've gotten over it now." Then a whole new sense of emptiness tumbles in on me. It sneaks up on my blind side. Sure, these times seem further apart now. But the depth of feeling at each occurrence is no less painful. But, being further apart doesn't make them easier. Sometimes I have a good time in between. Then I feel guilty. "I shouldn't be feeling this good," I tell myself. Dad and Elmer are dead, and I'm having a good time. Sometimes I tell myself, "They would want me to enjoy life," but these words seem hollow. Are they enjoying life? Where are they? Are they real? I am real, but I am embodied. Their bodies are buried in the cold ground this winter. I believe their spirits are somewhere. I wonder exactly where.

I try to recite the clichés about "being with the Lord" and "they are far happier now," but I'm not sure I always believe them with absolute confidence. Not that either would be anywhere but with God. But occasionally I wonder about the mystery of afterlife. Is there a trickle of doubt flowing among my faith?

But the alternative is much worse. Is there nothing after life? Are we a mere collection of molecules which evaporate at death? Is there no invisible world? Is all I have believed imaginary? Is living in vain? That doesn't make sense either. It is easier to believe the clichés. But belief is not always steady. Sometimes it is stronger, at other times weaker, and often it is mixed with doubt. I hope, over time, the trend is gradually up — toward a stronger faith. But my faith sometimes experiences a bear market.

Anger. I've heard of people getting angry with God. But I've never been. But I kind of feel that way sometimes. Not about Dad. His "time had come," I guess. Though that doesn't make it easier for me. But about my only brother, Elmer. His time hadn't. It's not fair. He was needed here. JoAn needs him, still does. And Scott needs him; high school seniors shouldn't be fatherless. And Kathy . . . what an enigma. Who ever knows what she's thinking? Quiet people like this often have even deeper needs than people who wear their emotions on their sleeves. She is about to graduate from Houghton, and is headed into life . . . if only she could talk to her dad about what to do next. But she can't. None of us can. God, it's not fair. I don't understand. God . . . Why? Why now? Why?

I've wondered a lot about what really killed Elmer? Was it really a heart attack? Or was it the church? Was the pressure as a college development man too great? What if he had simply done his job "good enough" like most everyone else does? Would he still be alive? He refused to coast. He gave 110%. He burned the candle at both ends. So do I. Was he a hero? Or was he a fool? What of my candle? Should I snuff out one end?

I've got to answer that letter from JoAn.

It's been lying here for several months now. What do you say to a young widow? Will it help? I dreaded opening it. Does she really want to hear back? Or is she just needing someone to listen . . . without talking back?

Calling is worse. I called several times right after Elmer died. She seemed grateful. But as time goes on, I sense I remind her of tragedy, not joy. Would she rather I not call at all? That's what I'm doing. Or rather, not doing. But I feel guilty about it.

What about my nephew and niece, Scott and Kathy? Maybe I remind them of their dad? Maybe when they hear my voice they choke up? Maybe they're mad at God and I remind them of Elmer's connection to the church? I wonder . . . I wish I could quickly explain all this to them. But I can't even explain it to myself.

My kids have been robbed. David and John need an uncle. Elmer didn't come very often . . . I can't remember any Christmas we spent together for a long time. But when he came the whole house buzzed. Whatever the kids were doing they stopped. At first to hear him make that crazy horn sound when he "beeped his nose." Later to hear him joke and laugh and solve every problem of the church and college. Will they remember him? Did they see him enough to catch what he was? Will they grow up positive people trying to be like their uncle? I hope so, but I'm afraid they didn't get enough exposure. Those times were full of laughter. That's why the kids were so attracted to the living room. When Elmer came, the house was full of laughter. I laughed too. I don't laugh enough anymore.

Elmer died like he wanted to. I remember when he met me at the airport in Allentown, when Dad was suffering so in his declining years. He shook his head and said, "He's slipping lower and lower, Keith." Then, after a moment of mutual silence he pointed to a concrete wall across from the entrance to the airport. "See that wall?" he asked. I nodded. "If that's the end of my life, I want to run all the way 'till I hit the wall."

He did.

It's hard to call Mom now. I call her anyway . . . almost every day. But it's hard. We chatter about details of her life, her church, the kids, my work, the weather, but we usually leave unsaid what we're really thinking. We don't talk about Dad or Elmer much. We sort of play this game together as if nothing had ever happened. Is this good? Or is it an unhealthy denial? I'm not sure. I just do it every day.

As time passes, grief worsens. I thought it was worst at first, then it got better with each passing month. In a way that's true, but in another way it misrepresents what really happens. It gets worse. Sometimes when I am driving out on the open lonely road, I just begin to cry . . . for no reason it seems. I know the reason. I'm lonely. I feel abandoned, isolated, alone. I want to be with my Dad . . . or my only brother. And I can't. Others forget. It's as if they hardly existed at all. I am asked, "Now, when was it that your dad died?" as if it was merely a fact on file . . . like my birth date or social security number. I answer mechanically and unemotionally. They probably think, "He's taking this well." I'm not. I am never far from these deaths. They are always near me, like the air I breathe. And a year later I don't feel much better. As everyone else forgets, I remember more.

I'm kind of getting over grief now. It's been a while since I even wrote about it. Kind of, that is. Sometimes I go for several days — even a week — without thinking of it. It's been well over a year. Some would probably say, "It's about time." They have already forgotten. "That's life, you know." My dad and brother have been assigned to some immaterial place called "history." They are in good company in the musty archives of church history. Life marches on. The Western Pennsylvania district, Penn Jersey District, The Stroudsburg Church, The Croswell Church, United Wesleyan, Central College . . . all roll on with their daily duties, as if these two men played minor roles somewhere far back in time.

Sometimes I too act this way. Elmer is a foggy memory . . . as if he is on some extended trip somewhere and will be home anytime now. And Dad is on his way to dialysis, and won't be back for a while yet. Reminiscences. Memories. Dreams. People of the past, who like old family pictures, are now identified with a name and a single anecdote. I'm getting over it I guess. I do this too.

I'll never really get over it. Not completely. It's not like a cold or the flu. You get sick, get better, then return to normal life as if you've never had it. Death is more like an amputation. When Dad had his legs cut off, he improved, got better, and was finally released from the hospital. His therapy enabled him to do all kinds of normal things again. When he was fitted with a prosthesis for each leg, he even learned to walk again. But things were never really the same. In a hundred little ways he was reminded of his missing legs every day. A prosthesis isn't a real leg. With "his legs on" others could hardly tell. He could tell. His legs were gone. Forever.

That's the way it is with Dad and Elmer. I'll really never "get over" their amputation from my life. I can put on a good front. "With my legs on" others think I've gotten over it. But really I haven't. I never will. In a hundred little ways I am reminded of these missing loved ones. They are gone forever. Amputated.

Earle Wilson talked to me about Elmer. Earle was close to Elmer. He said when he is alone traveling sometimes he breaks out into tears about Elmer's death. What was it about Elmer that makes a macho-type leader like Earle melt into tears more than a year after he's gone?

I hope someone cries for me when I'm dead.

Frankly, most of my grief is self-pity. I'm not really feeling bad for my dad and brother. I feel bad for me. I miss them for what they can do

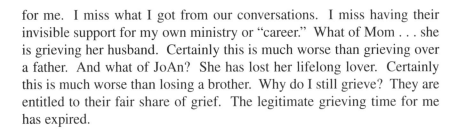
for me. I miss what I got from our conversations. I miss having their invisible support for my own ministry or "career." What of Mom . . . she is grieving her husband. Certainly this is much worse than grieving over a father. And what of JoAn? She has lost her lifelong lover. Certainly this is much worse than losing a brother. Why do I still grieve? They are entitled to their fair share of grief. The legitimate grieving time for me has expired.

Aloneness. That's what I feel most. Dad's gone. Elmer's gone. It's me alone now. Two people I could turn to are gone. Not that I turned to them enough when I could have. But I always knew I could. Now I feel alone, naked, exposed. I am stripped of some necessary, indefinable security I need. I wasn't even aware of how much I needed it. But it's gone. Forever. That's the trouble with death, it is forever.

Resurrection and hope. What is heaven like? I know there is life beyond the grave, but, not this kind of life. A much better life? I think not. Heaven is not an improved earth. It is totally different. Yes, better in a way, for we best understand it as superior by calling it "better." We suspect heaven is different from here in degree rather than kind. But heaven is not simply a souped-up earth. It is a totally different sphere of being.

I don't fully understand how a body can get resurrected and reunited with its spirit. I think they taught me how in seminary, but I've forgotten it. Actually, I've never thought much about the Resurrection, except at Easter. But it's been on my mind lately. I admit that sometimes I have glimmers of doubt.

But what's the alternative? If I do not believe the Resurrection, then the Bible is a myth and God cannot be trusted. If God cannot be trusted then life is a mockery . . . merely a high-level animal existence. This is no real alternative. Resurrection may be hard to understand, or even hard to believe at times, but it stretches the mind far less than nihilism. I believe in resurrection.

On that basis, I have hope. I yearn for a reunion somewhere, somehow, in that state of being the Bible calls heaven. Maybe then I'll have another of those quiet little chats with my dad. I'll have one of those laughing reunions with my brother. I don't know exactly where. I don't know how. But I choose to believe it will happen. If Christ was raised, shall not the rest of us rise? And if Christ be not raised, what

does anything else matter? I choose to believe in resurrection. It is a choice, not a feeling.

Why has grief so preoccupied me? The deaths of my father and brother had far more effect on me than they should have. Why? I think I know. It's not just because I miss them, though that was certainly the first factor. The reason my grief lasts is because it reminds me of my own mortality. It reminds me that every happy experience I create here, will someday be left behind. It reminds me that the closer I build relationships, the more difficult it will be to part. It reminds me that my exit date is out there lingering for me, waiting anxiously for me to catch up to it. Life is short . . . always shorter than you think it should be. This is the truth of death. Life is a mist. My life is a mist.

So what? What good comes out of all this? I don't know how many years I have left. I could have 50 years. I could have a month. What have I learned for these remaining years, more or less? What is the permanent influence of these two deaths on my life? What is the conclusion of the whole matter? After all, I can't keep looking backwards . . . what does God want to teach me through all this for the rest of my life?

It is clear. I remember that little plaque my mom hung right above my childhood bed. It was a sort of blue mirror with fancy lettering on it. I remember lying awake sometimes and reading it as a child. Funny how it has kept coming back to me these last two years. On that little plaque is the essence of my new commitment based on these deaths. It will be the new banner of my life:

> "Only one life, 'twill soon be past . . .
> Only what's done for Christ will last."

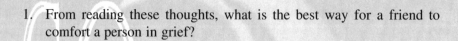

1. From reading these thoughts, what is the best way for a friend to comfort a person in grief?

2. Most people "get over it" quickly on the outside. What are the signs that a person is still grieving on the inside and needs solace?

3. What things are best left unsaid to a grieving person?

4. Can you pick out several stages (don't worry about the order) a grieving person might go through?

5. Where in the Bible — what passages, what stories — would you go to find solace in grief?

6. If the period of deep grief is often two years or so in length, who in your church might right now be feeling some of the thoughts outlined in the above journal?

7. What practical things could you do to offer solace to such a grieving person?

AFTERWORD

This book is about thinking. My conviction is that Christians are not idiot sheep who need to be told what to believe, but are people with minds and the ability to think through a subject and find the answers in God's Scriptures. However, this book will have failed in its purpose if it only inspires thought — the writer hopes that you will be driven to God's Holy Word to find answers to the perplexing questions we face.

If you have thought about some of these subjects, and your mind is turned toward the Scriptures for answers, then I will have succeeded. The Bible has guidance for the issues we face. Look there to find it. God will not fail us — He has given us the counsel for which we hunger.

A lot of our time in church is spent getting answers. This book has done some of that, but more importantly, it has asked questions. Why? Because the answers are in another book. The Bible. Go there and see!

Keith Drury

Spiritual Disciplines for Ordinary People

by Keith Drury

Serious Christians want to live holy lives and are always on the lookout for helps to spiritual maturity. If it's the little foxes that spoil the vines, it is everyday living that often gets in the way of our obedience. *Spiritual Disciplines for Ordinary People* offers answers for the problems related to making things right with others, forgiving those who have hurt you, battles with selfish ambition, pride and other areas of discipline in the spiritual life.

Each chapter includes a Bible study to help in the understanding and practical application of the subject. For classroom and small group settings, a complete leader's guide is available to help those in the pursuit of holiness.

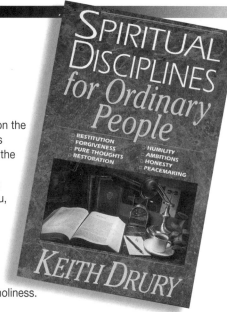

BKZ69	**Paperback**	**$9.95**
BKE50	**Spanish**	**$9.95**
BKM94	**Leader's Guide**	**$14.95**

(Prices at time of publication)

Money, Sex & Spiritual Power

by Keith Drury

These three "word-concepts" conjure up all kinds of images, experiences, and in some unfortunate cases, failure. Failure not only "out there" in a sinful secular society, but right inside the church! Frustrated, disillusioned secularists and saints alike want to know - and know now: **What's the answer?**

Ironically - yet hopefully, the heart of the solution lies right at the heart of the problem: **spiritual stewardship.** *Money, Sex & Spiritual Power* is a practical resource of biblical insight and "spiritual common sense" to help each of us deal with these topics.

| BKR82 | **Paperback** | **$7.95** |
| BKR81 | **Leader's Guide** | **$14.95** |

(Prices at time of publication)

WESLEYAN PUBLISHING HOUSE
P.O. Box 50434
Indianapolis, IN 46250-0434

To Order Call:
800-4 WESLEY
(800-493-7539)